Resistance in an Amazonian Community

RESISTANCE IN AN AMAZONIAN COMMUNITY

Huaorani Organizing against the Global Economy

Lawrence Ziegler-Otero

Berghahn Books
New York • Oxford

Published in 2004 by

Berghahn Books

www.berghahnbooks.com

©2004 Lawrence Ziegler-Otero
First paperback edition published in 2007

Library of Congress Cataloging-in-Publication Data

Ziegler-Otero, Lawrence.
  Resistance in an Amazonian community : Huaorani organizing against the global community /
Lawrence Ziegler-Otero.
    p. cm.
  Includes bibliographical references and index.
  ISBN 1-57181-448-5 (hbk) -- ISBN 1-84545-306-9 (pbk)
    1. Organización de las Nacionalidades Indígenas de la Amazonia Ecuatoriana--History.
  2. Huao Indians--Politics and government.. 3. Huao Indians--Civil rights. 4. Huao
  Indians--Government relations. 5. Protest movements--Ecuador. 6. Self-determination,
  National--Ecuador. 7. Indians, Treatment of--Ecuador. 8. Ecuador--Race relations. 9.
  Ecuador--Politics and government. 10. Ecuador--Social policy. I. Title.

F3722.1.H83Z54 2004
986.6'400498--dc21   2003051811

British Library Cataloguing in Publication Data

A catalogue record for this book is available from the British Library

Printed in the United States on acid-free paper

ISBN-10: 1-57181-448-5   ISBN-13: 978-1-57181-448-7   hardback
ISBN-10: 1-84545-306-9   ISBN-13: 978-1-84545-306-0   paperback

CONTENTS

ACKNOWLEDGEMENTS

It is of course a cliché to state that a book or other large undertaking "would not have been possible without the support of …" But like many clichés, it is often repeated precisely because of its fundamental underlying truth. While this work is a product of my years of research, it is also very much a product of ongoing conversations with my colleagues, friends, family, and students. At their best, these conversations have stimulated my thinking, challenging me to continually rethink what I thought were settled ideas and arguments.

I would like to thank my academic colleagues in the U.S.: Thomas Patterson, Anthony Ranere, Elmer Miller, Kathy Walker, Kenneth Kensinger, and Terry Turner, as well as the late Peter Rigby. In Ecuador, where I received invaluable assistance as well as moral support from FLACSO in Quito, I would like to thank Flica Barclay and Francisco Carrion of FLACSO, Andy Drumm, Javier Grijalva, Delaney Kellon, and Leonardo Viteri. I am also grateful to my friends Mark DeBevoise and John Caroulis who read and commented on previous versions of this work.

The people at Berghahn Books have been wonderful to work with, including Marion Berghahn, Maria Reyes, and Jaime Taber, a truly amazing copy editor who has made me sound better than I deserve.

Next come thanks to my family, who have had to put up with the entire process: my wife, Wanda Otero-Ziegler, who as usual has exhibited patience and support above and beyond the call; my daughter Rosa Jacqueline Faith Ziegler, who has seemingly grown up while being told "Daddy is writing"; and my mother Jacqueline C. Ziegler, for her gentle encouragement to "get it done."

In the end, of course, the greatest debt is owed to the activists of ONHAE and to the Huaorani people. I was granted access, friendship, and support that will take me a lifetime to repay. Their bravery, humor, and gentility are my inspiration. Ultimately it is to the Huaorani and their continuing struggle for survival that this work is dedicated.

INTRODUCTION

In 1990 the Huaorani people of eastern Ecuador formed the *Organización de las Nacionalidades Indígenas de la Amazonia Ecuatoriana* or ONHAE. The group of young, Spanish-literate men who initiated this step wanted an organization that could speak for the Huaorani in dealings with the multinational oil companies, missionaries, and state agencies that were increasingly threatening Huaorani territory and autonomy. In founding a nongovernmental organization (NGO), the Huaorani were emulating the organizational processes of the Shuar (Jívaro), Quichua, and Siona-Secoya groups, and joining with them in provincial, regional, and national confederations. This represented a dramatic step outside of Huaorani cultural practices and necessitated the adoption of notions of contract, government, democracy, and hierarchical power prevalent in western capitalist societies.

The organization thus formed has found itself positioned among and within a plethora of competing interests, powers, and ideologies. Missionaries, oil companies, environmentalists, and other indigenous organizations have all tried to co-opt, manipulate, or silence ONHAE. The organization's leaders have been accused of corruption, threatened, condemned as "communists," and beguiled with gifts and attention designed to influence them. They have signed agreements with the Ecuadorian state and the oil companies, in apparent contradiction of their organizational positions and public statements.

Notes for this section can be found on page 24.

The preceding narrative raises a number of important questions. Why did an organization whose primary purpose at the time of its founding was to block the oil development of Huaorani territory sign not just one but a series of legally binding contracts permitting exactly such oil exploration? How have non-Huaorani used Huaorani cultural practices to manipulate the leaders of ONHAE? How has the creation of such an organization affected Huaorani cultural practices, and how have the leaders of ONHAE been able to interact with the representatives and institutions of a capitalist nation state and international economy? Finally, what can be learned from the experiences of ONHAE–what are the special pitfalls facing traditionally egalitarian societies when they try to organize?

This study examines ONHAE, the organization and its leaders, by placing them within the multiple and interpenetrating contexts in which they are forced to operate. By forming a representative organization, one legally authorized to speak for the Huaorani people, the founders of the group created an identifiable nexus of power within the traditionally acephalous Huaorani culture. The oil companies, the missionaries, and the state were subsequently able to target this small, inexperienced leadership cadre in their continuous efforts to influence and suborn ONHAE policy. Thus, by abandoning the traditionally diffuse decision making processes of Huaorani culture, a seemingly progressive and logical step, the very formation of an organization dedicated to struggle rendered that organization an instrument of forced assimilation, capitalist penetration, and the loss of independence of another of the world's indigenous peoples.

This research is important for anthropology in a number of ways. Currently, in the wake of the controversy sparked by Tierney's critical appraisal of the work of Napoleon Chagnon and others, anthropology is in the midst of a reappraisal of its role in the struggle for indigenous autonomy and self-determination. The discipline of anthropology has a long-standing relationship with indigenous societies around the world and, I believe, a moral and ethical obligation to serve as an advocate for indigenous rights. This commitment has been echoed by many of those working with what Richard Lee (2000) has called "the small peoples" (cf. Rabben

1998, esp. 27-41; Sponsel 1995: 274-83; Warren 1998: xi-xv). The Declaration of Barbados (quoted in Sponsel 1995: 275) calls on anthropologists to reject false notions of scientistic "neutrality" in favor of active support for indigenous rights and activism. Sponsel (1995: 277-79) states:

> *The rights to life, movement, land, resources, food, shelter, health care, education, culture, language, religion and self-determination are basic for the survival, adaptation, and welfare of indigenes in Amazonia.* Ecological anthropologists can help document, defend, and promote these needs in traditional and acculturated societies. [Italics in original.]

The Actors

Throughout this work the activities of a number of categories of "actors" will be analyzed. These include the Huaorani themselves, the oil companies, the missionaries, the other indigenous organizations in the territory, and the environmentalists. The following is intended to serve as a brief introduction to these principal actors.

The Huaorani are a comparatively isolated group numbering between 1,800 and 2,000 individuals scattered over a territory roughly the size of Puerto Rico. They make their living as hunters, gatherers, and horticulturists, although a small number have taken wage work with the oil companies for brief periods and some have served briefly in the Ecuadorian military. Until the early 1960s there was no sustained peaceful contact between the Huaorani and the rest of Ecuadorian society. The Huaorani were feared in the region, and frequently killed any non-Huaorani that entered their territory. Coincidental with the decision to exploit the oil reserves in the Ecuadorian Amazon, during the 1950s, North American evangelical missionaries mounted a concerted campaign to missionize the Huaorani.

When a group of four of these missionaries was killed ("martyred," in the language of the missionaries) by Huaorani warriors in 1956, the world's attention was focused on this small group. Missionization finally took place in the 1960's, and the Huaorani are only now beginning to reassert their cultural identity in independent ways.

I will use the word "isolated" in connection with the Huaorani although it is a word that has fallen out of favor with anthropologists today. Of course there was always contact between the Huaorani and surrounding groups even when that contact largely consisted of mutual avoidance. Nevertheless, the relative lack of friendly or trading contacts, the rarity of intermarriage, and the continuing geographic separation of the Huaorani all speak to an isolation that is real if not absolute.

The second principal actor in this discussion is the oil interests. As will be discussed in detail, North American, European, and South American oil companies have steadily increased their operations in the *oriente*[1] throughout the last forty years. Sustained activity within Huaorani territory is a much more recent phenomenon. Only since the 1980s has there been sustained, large-scale exploitation of the oil reserves in Huaorani lands. All of the *oriente* has been divided into numbered oil exploration/exploitation blocks that have been auctioned off by the Ecuadorian state to a variety of different oil companies. The section that has the largest chunk of Huaorani territory is Block 16. At the time of this research the oil rights to Block 16 belonged to Maxus Energy, a Houston-based oil company. Since then, Maxus has itself been purchased by YPF, the private oil corporation formed by the privatization of the state-owned Argentinian oil company. One particular group within the Maxus organization, the Department of Community Relations, has the responsibility of negotiating with the Huaorani. Milton Ortega, a self-proclaimed anthropologist and the head of this department in Ecuador at the time of my fieldwork, is in almost daily contact with each of the leaders of ONHAE.

American missionaries play a tremendously important role in Huaorani society. Beginning in the 1950s the Huaorani became a favorite target of North American evangelical Christian missionaries. These right wing, fundamentalist, missionaries, originally affiliated with the Summer Institute of Linguistics, actively promote the Huaorani's incorporation within capitalist relations of production and exchange. As will be discussed in detail, the evangelicals were granted administrative control of an area known as the "Protectorate"–a reservation that eventually contained a majority of the Huaorani population. The missionaries have maintained close and friendly relationships with the oil companies doing business in Huaorani territory.

Another principal player in the development of ONHAE is the organized indigenous movement. Ecuador has a unique and long history of formal organization by indigenous peoples. In the 1960s the Shuar (Jívaro) formed the Federación de Centros Shuar. In the years since nearly every indigenous group in Ecuador has formed at least one major ethnic federation. These different federations, in turn, have joined together in regional Amazonian (CONFENIAE) and national (CONAIE) alliances.[2] These movements have become articulated with socialist and labor movements within Ecuador through shifting and strategic alliances, although never with any of the short-lived guerrilla movements of the 1960s. The indigenous movement has wielded substantial power in Ecuadorian political life for many years (so much so that efforts have been made by the right to co-opt or replace the movement) and at the time of my fieldwork mounted its first major foray into national electoral politics, joining with Nuevo Pais, a democratic socialist party and a member of the Socialist International, to form Pachakutik, a national indigenous/socialist political party. Although dismissed by the major pundits as a minor party, Pachakutik eventually came in a strong third place out of more than twenty slates competing in the 1996 national election, and has become the chief voice of opposition in the national congress after playing a major role in the subsequent popular revolt that unseated *Rolodista* President Abdala Bucaram in 1997-98.

The last "actors" in the Huaorani organizational saga are the environmentalists, who see themselves as the Huaorani's allies in struggle. This is a diverse group that includes national Ecuadorian environmental groups (Acción Ecológica, Amazonia por la Vida, and others) as well as international groups, most notably the San Francisco based Rainforest Action Network and the Danish Ibis Foundation. Certain individual environmentalists, most notably Joe Kane, Andy Drumm, and Judith Kimmerling, are also a part of this milieu. These groups have sought contacts and cooperation with ONHAE and its leaders, provided funding to the organization, and pressured the leadership of ONHAE to reduce or eliminate their contact with and dependence on the oil companies. The environmentalists do not see themselves as another interested outside group putting pressure on the Huaorani leadership; rather, they see themselves as the group's allies in a unilateral struggle against the oil companies and feel betrayed at each new agreement or exchange with the companies.

The Question of Organizing

The case of the Huaorani takes on enormous importance in the study of indigenous peoples and human rights when placed within the context of capitalist expansion, globalization, and the destruction of tropical rainforests. Most, if not all, of the world's indigenous peoples are facing the threat of cultural or actual annihilation through contact with capitalism. Many groups both in Latin America and in the rest of the world have begun the process of organization and are attempting to assert their right to some form of self-determination through the channels presented by governments and supergovernmental institutions. MacDonald (1995b) has dubbed this the "new institutionalism." For many, this is their first exposure to such a world, and their attempts to organize have been hampered by their unfamiliarity with the forms of protest, negotiation, development, and contract with which they must deal.

The case of the Huaorani is not unique among indigenous peoples. As the tendrils of global capitalism penetrate ever further into what were previously the most remote corners of the earth, indigenous groups everywhere are confronted by what is for them a new and totalizing system of economic and social life. Once a culture has been destroyed there is no way to bring it back to life, and the shocked and devastated descendants of a society thus destroyed will not recover, psychically or materially, for many generations if ever. In order to preserve any semblance of true cultural self-determination, indigenous peoples must be capable of negotiating the inevitable conflicts and must be able to maintain a safe space in which to adopt or reject elements of the system that has arrived on their doorstep. One way to do this is to organize in such a way that their organizations act not as a "bridge" between two cultures, but as a tool of diplomacy between two competing sets of cultural practices. But organizing by subaltern groups is an activity inevitably fraught with peril. At worst, it can mean death or prison for leaders and reprisals against the groups' members. Even if such dramatic consequences are avoided, the organizations must contend with subornation, co-optation, careerism, and simple ineffectiveness. ONHAE provides an important case study to be considered by other indigenous groups and those who advocate on their behalf.

In this introductory section I will first locate the Huaorani experience within the broad framework of international capitalism. Second, I will attempt to place ONHAE, the organization itself, within a similarly broad economic, historical, and organizational framework. Finally, I will attempt to draw conclusions about such organizing efforts, the challenges they face, and their prospects for success.

The Huaorani in the "Global" Economy

Any analysis of the Huaorani's organizing efforts must first locate the Huaorani themselves within the national, regional, and world economies. The Huaorani are a pre-capitalist society, what Barbara Bradby (1980) calls a "natural economy." As will be discussed in Chapter 1, land and all means of production are "owned" communally and there is no sense of individual private property. The forest and "wild" products are not owned or identified with any particular group or community, while gardens, *chonta* palms (peach palms), and other sites of production requiring the intervention of humans are owned by the respective *nanicabo* ("longhouse") groups for as long as the groups remain in a given area. The forest land is not a single entity, nor is it in any sense "property"; it is instead understood by the Huaorani as a system of interpenetrating rights, responsibilities and traditions.

Capitalism has been called a "totalizing" economic system because of its tendency to overwhelm and destroy other (precapitalist) economic formations as it advances. In practice, however, capitalism, although invariably emerging as the *dominant* mode of production, can frequently co-exist over time with other precapitalist modes of production. By "dominant mode of production" I mean two things: first, that in a direct conflict of interest between capitalists and participants in precapitalist economic formations, the capitalists will always be able to bring sufficient pressure to resolve the conflict in their favor; and second, that the exchange or market value of capitalist economic activity will quickly over-shadow the relative importance of noncapitalist economic activity. This phenomenon has been called the "articulation of modes of production" (Nugent 1993; Patterson 1999; Wolpe 1980; Wood 1983;). Wood (1983: 259-64), referring to the "dual character of the frontier," states that "capitalist and non-capitalist social relations co-exist, not in isolation from one another, but as interrelated aspects of the frontier economy." The two (or more) different pro-ductive systems do not merely exist in proximity to one another; rather, they must interact effectively and there must be a transfer of value from one to the other. This interaction is in a continual process of negotiation, a process in which capitalist interests, in the end, will always have more weight and power. The articulation that takes place is not only economic, but ideological as well (Murato-rio 1981: 37-39). Patterson (1999: 135-6) relying on P. Rey, stresses the violent nature of this articulation, and sees it as part of an inex-orable process of the extension of the hegemony of capitalist pro-duction. In *The Communist Manifesto*, Marx (1967: 134-35) himself presents capitalism as a force that totally eliminates precapitalist economic formations when he says: "The bourgeoisie, wherever it has got the upper hand, has put an end to all feudal, patriarchal, idyllic relations." However, these depictions of capitalistic expan-sion are overly deterministic. The trajectory of capitalist expansion is itself a dialectical process and must not be viewed as inevitable, teleological, or irreversible. So-called pre-capitalist productive forms not only survive extended periods of articulation with capi-talism, they may also reappear within the core countries themselves as the economically disenfranchised seek a livelihood through the "gathering" of refuse or self-sufficient agriculture. In either case, the portion of the productive enterprise that may remain in the pre-capitalist sector of economic activity is distinguishable by its con-tinuing irrelevance to the fundamental operations of the capitalist productive process. As stated by Muratorio (1981: 39):

> [C]apitalist expansion and its penetration in the rural areas of the third world has not been universally successful, nor even a smooth and irreversible process, but rather a convergence of contradictory forces. Complex forms of articulation involving both persistence and destruction reflect a continuous dialectic between capitalism and previous economic formations.

Capitalism requires different things from its interaction with precapitalist economic formations at different stages of its development and in different geographical and historical circumstances. These needs may include land (e.g. the enclosures in England), labor, or raw materials (lumber, minerals, etc.) (Bradby 1980: 94-99).

Inherent in the articulation of modes of production in an economic and material sense is the concomitant articulation of ideologies. As discussed by Muratorio (1981: 38-41), this entails the persistence of ideological constructs linked to precapitalist social formations, and the integration of these ideological systems with those encouraged or required by the emergent capitalist ruling classes. These shifting ideologies provide rationalization and psychological support for capitalist-driven changes while helping to disguise them or articulate the new practices with the old.

Looking now at the Huaorani, we find a geographically and historically isolated group numbering no more than two thousand individuals spread out over a vast area of land. The "primitive communism" of the Huaorani represents no threat to the development of capitalist relations of production in Ecuador or the Amazon region. The mode of production of Huaorani society is cooperative, lineage based, and self-sufficient in the sense of "self subsistence" expressed by Emmanuel Terray (1972: 152). Their land remains relatively inaccessible, and thus of little value to capitalist agriculture. Even if roads were to be constructed, the continuing difficulties in transportation (over the Andes) would impede effective agricultural exploitation of the region. The Huaorani people themselves do not represent any significant potential pool of labor power, except for certain very specialized short-term work in the forest.

At this moment the only thing that the Huaorani "have" that is important to capitalist development is crude oil deposits under their territory. As Eduardo Galeano (1997: 217) puts it: "The North American economy needs Latin America's minerals like lungs need the air." Given the expense and logistical difficulties involved in establishing any sort of permanent capitalist infrastructure, and the nearly total absence of either a pool of labor or investment capital, it seems unlikely that the Ecuadorian Amazon (or at least Huaorani territory) will experience the violent transformation to capitalist social relations anytime soon. Intensive capitalist penetration of the territory, for the moment, is likely to be instead confined to the development of extractive industries with a high organic composition of capital.

This does not mean that such penetration does not bring with it agents of social transformation. Both the missionaries, acting (whether intentionally or not) as agents of westernization and capitalism, and the Ecuadorian state, with its adoption of the paradigm of regional "development," including education and infrastructure improvements, inculcate capitalist ideology and encourage social and economic practices characteristic of capitalist economic relations. But the distinction here has to do not with whether or not such transformative agents are indeed active in the territory (or in others similarly situated); rather, it is a matter of extent and intensity. It is imperative to global capitalist interests that the oil underlying Huaorani land be extracted; it is not, however, equally imperative that the Huaorani people themselves become available as wage laborers, or that the land, if not destroyed by the very process of oil extraction, be incorporated into the worldwide system of agricultural production and markets. As stated by Bradby (1980: 126):

> [C]apital is perfectly indifferent to what happens in the natural economy. If capital's main interest in the Peruvian jungle is in the land and raw materials, then there is no reason why it should have any interest in what happens to the Indians, as long as they get out of the way. There are two ways of getting them out of the way: one is the process I have described in Peru, which commits no greater and no lesser sin than the destruction of an ancient culture; the other is faster accomplished and consists in the physical extermination of Indians. ...

What this distinction means for the Huaorani is that a space may exist in which the very process of their incorporation into the capitalist world is open to an ongoing process of negotiation. It may mean that some of the brutality that usually accompanies such capitalist expansion may be mitigated or vitiated, and that a degree of cultural autonomy may be maintained through the efforts of the newly emerging ethnic entrepreneurs.

Ethnic Identity and Ethnogenesis

A second component necessary to understanding the Huaorani organization and the location of the Huaorani people in the context of global development is the question of ethnic identity and cohesiveness. Huaorani identity has always been defined in relation to *cowode*, or non-Huaorani, but this consciousness of the ethnic "other" does not necessarily imply the existence of a broader ethnic identity. In fact, the word "Huaorani," which means "people," is traditionally only used for kin. Unrelated or distantly related speakers of Huao Terero are properly referred to as *huarani*, which means "other people." Their consciousness of a more complex identity, rooted in specific cultural practices and delineated along lines laid out and accepted by both themselves and by Ecuadorian society, is a post-contact phenomenon. Robarchek and Robarchek (1998) see the formation of ONHAE as an important marker of the development of a distinct ethnic identity as "Huaorani":

> Of course, the strongest and most explicit manifestation of this creation of an ethnic identity is in the formation of ONHAE. This reflects a conscious and deliberate attempt to create a single "nation" from the dispersed kindreds and regional bands.

Patterson (1999: 67) has defined ethnogenesis as the realization and conceptualization of commonality occurring when "people who occupied the same position in a stratified society began to recognize that they had a shared identity." This recognition of traits shared with those similarly situated has been possible only since the violent penetration and subsequent juxtaposition of the Huaorani culture with western, Quichua, and mestizo cultural milieus. In addition to ONHAE, the creation of a school system encompassing most of the Huaorani communities, soccer leagues, and radio communication have also been factors contributing to a "pan-Huaorani" consciousness. Turner (1995: 5), discussing changes in ethnic consciousness that came about in conjunction with the formation of a Kayapo indigenous organization speaks of the "reassertion and redefinition of ethnic identity, accompanied by the revaluation and more or less creative reinvention of indigenous culture."

Organizations of Amazonian Indigenous Peoples

Organizations of indigenous peoples in the Amazon Basin are not a new phenomenon. The Federación Shuar was first formed in the 1960s, and by the 1980s indigenous groups throughout the region had formed ethno-political organizations. Wherever there exist class-stratified social structures, there is oppression that will engender resistance. The forms that the resistance can take are myriad, from spontaneous revolts to labor unions and political organizations, revolutionary movements, or what James Scott (1990) has called "the everyday forms" of resistance–dissembling, ridicule, uncooperativeness, etc. Broadly based mass organizations have taken on ever greater importance in the strategies of Latin American progressives. Not just organizations of indigenous peoples, but unions of women, peasants, workers, and others have replaced vanguardism among many progressive movements in the region (Chinchilla 1992: 48-50).

In Ecuador in particular, indigenous groups have formed more or less formal, institutional organizations along perceived ethnic lines, and these groups in turn have joined together in regional and national federations created (ostensibly) to represent, defend, and support the interests of the indigenous populations of the country. This contrasts with indigenous support for armed guerrilla groups in neighboring Colombia and Peru. Ecuador has led the region in the establishment of these ethnic organizations, which wield more power there than in any other Amazonian nation, as evidenced by the relative success of Pachakutik in national politics and by the concessions wrung from the government and the ruling class by the organizations (Macdonald 1995B). Selverston (1995: 131) argues effectively that the

> indigenous movement [has] created a political space for the indigenous population by making "cultural" demands on the political

system.... Through their cultural battles, and in particular through bilingual education, the indigenous movement has created a strong organizational base that is now an important actor in the national political arena.

Tarrow (1994) suggests that while organizations such as these may draw on local or ethnic group symbols in their efforts to define themselves, the organizational impetus usually comes from the experience and observed history of other groups in analogous situations. Outside influences that have shaped the development of the Huaorani organization have included progressive Catholic clergy, environmentalists, and anthropologists,[3] but most important has been the influence and example of the organizations representing other indigenous groups in the region. It is notable as well that this movement has succeeded in uniting disparate groups with a long history of hostility among them and forging this coalition into an effective force in national (and at times international) politics. At the same time the Ecuadorian indigenous movement has experienced grave failures, corruption, and internal power struggles.

It is important that the Huaorani, and other Ecuadorian indigenous groups, selected a more or less formal NGO as a means of protecting their rights. They did not resort to forms of resistance rooted in the supernatural, such as the "John Frum" cargo cults of Melanesia (Worsley 1968) or the Ghost Dance movement of nineteenth-century native North Americans. Nor did they involve themselves in violent forms of resistance, either independently (as was Huaorani practice before missionization) or as part of the Eloy Alfaro or other guerrilla movements. Alternatively, in the absence of more formal resistance movements, the Huaorani could have resorted to what Scott (1990) calls "everyday forms" of resistance. Scott, who rejects the idea of ideological hegemony and generally sees organizing and struggle by subaltern groups as both futile and dangerous, has made an important contribution to resistance theory by properly identifying many activities as "resistance" insofar as they represent some form of oppositional behavior, albeit ineffective. Instead the generation of young Huaorani men who founded ONHAE chose to create an organization that would be designed to operate, in large part, in a cultural setting wholly alien to the Huaorani experience.

By choosing an institutional response, the founders of ONHAE placed themselves inside the "game" of national and international politics and government. In order to succeed through this sort of institutional strategy, their organization had to achieve some sort of parity or equality with the opposing forces. ONHAE has attained a certain degree of legitimacy through its association with regional and national federations of indigenous organizations and through a frequently tenuous alliance with national and international environmentalist organizations, which have been able to gain a significant amount of publicity both in Ecuador and in the U.S. and Europe.

From the beginning, ONHAE was to operate as a negotiating entity mediating between the oil companies, the state, the missionaries, and the Huaorani themselves. For the Huaorani, most of whom still fail to differentiate between the different oil companies, and who still have only a very limited and culturally alienated understanding of what a contract is, and whose command of Spanish remains somewhat limited, this was a remarkable decision. That they chose such a course can be partly explained by the example of the already extant indigenous organizations, and the influence of Ecuadorian environmentalists and rights activists. The oil companies, the state, and the environmentalists have all tried to co-opt the leadership cadre of ONHAE. Using gifts and making promises, all have tried (sometimes successfully) to shape Huaorani policy. The leadership of ONHAE, by balancing these mutually hostile actors, has brought substantial quantities of goods to the communities. Another question, however, is the extent to which such balancing is conscious and deliberate.

The Huaorani in the Context of Amazonian Development

Ethnic federations are meant to be advocacy organizations. But advocacy for what purpose–for what ultimate goal? Environmentalists endorse the organizations as long as they steadfastly reject "development" in any form, but can become highly critical of the federations if they try to benefit from or regulate development (see Macdonald 1995B; Ramos 1994). In representing indigenous peoples, organizations such as ONHAE must try to negotiate the path that seems to provide the most benefit for their communities. Gray (1997: 244-47) suggests a form of autochthonous (self-directed) development, which he describes as endogenous, need oriented, and ecologically sound. But in the Huaorani case, such a course is not realistic. With Ecuador now in a relation of debt peonage to the United States and international banking institutions, the presence of oil under Huaorani territory has become an irresistible force. Evaluation of ONHAE's effectiveness must properly situate the organization in its relation to oil, environmentalism, colonization, missionization, and national identity. In fact, one of the major successes of ONHAE is precisely its independence–rather than be dominated by any one interested outside party (like the missionaries in the past), the Huaorani have embarked on a balancing act that calls for the constant negotiation of their position vis a vis each of the other groups. Siracusa (1996: 254) has made similar observations with regard to both ONHAE and the Federación Shuar.

Much can also be learned from the comparison of ONHAE with other indigenous groups and their experience of organization. The experience of the Kayapo in the central Brazilian Amazon, as recorded by Terence Turner (1995) differs from that of the Huaorani in significant ways. First, the Kayapo leaders have fallen into a more brazen, personal corruption, spending money on town houses, luxury goods, and prostitutes, while the Huaorani have so far avoided this sort of personal aggrandizement. The second major difference between the Kayapo and Huaorani experiences is the form of capital involved in the penetration of their territory. Although both groups face "extractive" capital, this single form of capital must be subdivided by the type of capital investment required–the "organic composition" of capital.

The most significant difference between the Kayapo and Huaorani organizational experiences has to do with the nature of the industries with which they are confronted. Capitalist penetration of the Amazon is being driven by the extractive industries–mining (gold, uranium), logging, oil, and others. But while these industries all share certain traits as extractive capitalist enterprises, there is a marked difference between them in the scope of investment in machinery and infrastructure, the amount of labor power required on-site, and the extent of government and international scrutiny and regulation. The first two of these elements can be called the organic composition of capital; only relatively large, established companies could hope to purchase oil rights and successfully exploit them. In contrast, small-scale gold mining or logging operations can be conducted with very little capital. In Kayapo territory the penetration of capitalist extractive industry has come in the form of gold mining and logging. These can both be carried out by any of a large number of entrepreneurs, many of whom, if denied legal access to the site, are willing to operate illegally or secretly. This of course is not possible for the oil industry. The Kayapo leaders are confronting a form of capital that is labor intensive, attracts many small capitalists, and is largely unregulated by the government. Many of the capitalists operating in Kayapo lands are national (Brazilian) and do not wield the economic or political power of multinational oil companies. This difference means that the Huaorani are facing a more sophisticated and better placed foe, one that is able to count on the unshakable support of the Ecuadorian state in its dealings with indigenous people.

At the same time, the oil companies are susceptible to pressures that would not have any effect on a tiny mining or logging operation. Publicity campaigns by international environmental and rights groups can have at least some short-term effects on the policies and behaviors of the oil companies, as evidenced by the withdrawal of Conoco from Block 16. Even Maxus, now a part of the Argentine company YPF (formerly the state-run oil company of Argentina, now privatized), is extremely sensitive to criticism of its policies toward the Huaorani and attempts to conceal its depredations behind the veil of negotiations and *convenios* with ONHAE.

Another example of capitalist penetration is provided by David Price's account of the Brazilian Nambiquara. In this case capitalist penetration was accomplished not by large scale industries, extractive or otherwise, but through highway construction and a deliberate policy of colonization. Such policies are common in Amazonia, and have been undertaken in parts of Ecuador as well (Mera and Montaño 1984). In such cases the goals of the promoters are the "modernization" of the region and the opening up of the region to capitalist agriculture, as well as a temporary concealment of the contradictions caused by the presence of a large mass of landless peasants with no place within the fledging institutions of capitalist production in the peripheral nations. It has also been suggested that the colonists' invasion of territory serves to mask or "clean" (*sanear*) the activities of destructive, extractive industries since the space they are operating in is already settled and not "pristine" (Villamil 1995: 341-42). But the first stages of this development are not accompanied by the establishment of capitalist relations of production but by the extension of a peasant economy built on a base of primitive accumulation, and the subsequent development of merchant capitalism in the region. Price saw the Nambiquara as completely incapable of effective negotiation with the "developed" economic forces of Brazil and sought ways to personally intervene on their behalf (1989: 32-40).

Another factor operating to enhance the effectiveness of ONHAE within Ecuador, particularly in its dealings with the Ecuadorian state, is the relative strength of the national indigenous movement. The nationally based Confederación de Nacionalidades Indígenas del Ecuador (CONAIE) and the regional Confederación de las Nacionalidades Indígenas de la Amazonia Ecuadoriana (CONFENIAE) represent perhaps one-third of the national population. They have demonstrated their ability to mobilize their members through national strikes, marches, and their support, since 1996, for the Pachakutik political movement. ONHAE may represent only a small number of people scattered throughout a vast forest, but when they speak with the guidance and support of the rest of the indigenous movement, the government must at least listen.

Another factor to consider in evaluating the effectiveness of ONHAE is the extent to which it reflects the will and desires of the Huaorani people. The indigenous movement in Ecuador is notable for having been largely led and directed throughout its existence by autochthonous leaders. Founders of the movement may have drawn their inspiration from outside examples, but the movement has been led by native Ecuadorians. This contrasts with Brazil, where many of the "indigenist" NGOs are in fact led by non-native Brazilians (Maybury-Lewis 1997: 28; Ramos 1994). Further important support for (at least well known) Brazilian indigenous people comes from international organizations (Maybury-Lewis 1997: 24-

30). However, there is an important parallel between the attitude toward indigenous peoples' organizations by non-native activists described by Ramos (1994) and the experience of the Ecuadorian indigenist movement. Many "friends of the Indian" see a natural environmentalist, a spiritual protector of the forest–really an updated version of the "noble savage" (cf. Acción Ecologica 1994: 153-83; Delgado 1996). ONHAE, the Organización de los Pueblos Indígenas de Pastaza (OPIP), and other indigenous organizations work with and receive support and guidance from environmental and progressive organizations based in Ecuador. Ramos (1994: 157) describes the reaction of the leaders of non-native led NGOs who felt betrayed by certain decisions and accommodations made by the leaders:

> After having helped the Indians with fund-raising and organization of the event, they claimed the right to tell them what was right and wrong, who were the good guys and the bad guys. Several whites said they had been betrayed by the Indian leaders who trampled on their political principles. The message inserted into such a reaction could be read–and actually was by some observers–as this: we, whites, help you, Indians, and in turn you, Indians, must do what we, whites, think is correct.

The Huaorani leaders must work within the context of a constant tension between the missionaries and oil companies on the one hand, and the national and international environmentalists, human rights, and progressive organizations on the other. Each interest group has an agenda and a preferred course of action for indigenous policy. More significantly, each group in turn feels that if they have provided support for the organization they have some right to push the leaders toward that organization's preferred policies. This was manifested in the pressure brought to bear on the leaders of ONHAE when they received funding for their annual assembly from the Rainforest Action Network, and when they accepted money from Maxus for schools or Huaorani hospital bills. Much of what the ONHAE leaders must do is to choose between the contradictory policy possibilities being promoted by different "friends" of the Huaorani–each of whom is providing material support for the organization and the communities.

The views of the "Indian" implicit in the attitudes of indigenist support organizations and in the discourse of environmental groups are varied, but none of them allow indigenous people their full stature as complex human beings. Ramos (1994: 164) describes the views of Brazilian non-indigenous led environmental NGOs in this way:

> [E]nvironmental NGOs tend to regard the Indians from opposing viewpoints: one sees them as predators and therefore excludes from ecologically protected areas, even at the cost of eviction. The other naturalizes the Indian, reducing him to yet another endangered species, or to the role of custodian of nature.

The Huaorani in particular, because of their history of violence (albeit ultimately defensive) toward non-Huaorani and because of their successful resistance to sustained contact until relatively recently, are among a select group of indigenous peoples viewed in popular discourse as somehow more "authentic." This has also been true of the Shuar (Jívaro) of Ecuador (Taylor 1994), the Yanomami (Ramos 1994), and the Kayapo of Brazil (Turner 1995). The "exotic" image of the Huaorani has been fed both by the missionary literature (see for example Elliot 1958, 1966; Hitt 1975; Jackson and Jackson 1997) and by what I will loosely categorize as the "environmentalist" literature (Broennimann 1981; Kane 1993, 1995, etc.). This is one of the things that have led to tourists' interest in the Huaorani, and perhaps contributed to the intense interest in the Huaorani people on the part of at least some of the international and national environmental groups.

It is also true, however, that the current interest in the Amazon rainforest and the worldwide attention being paid to the indigenous peoples of the Amazon have provided the Huaorani and other similarly situated Amazonian populations with an opportunity to influence public policy and to attract publicity.[4] Just as Gandhi was able to achieve Indian independence in part because of the peculiar moral sensibilities of the English middle class at mid century, so too, the case of the Huaorani has had a particular appeal to environmentalists in the U.S. and western Europe. Books and articles by Joe Kane (1993, 1995), films such as Christopher Walker's Trinkets and Beads (1996), and active support by North American environmental groups (notably the Rainforest Action Network) have fueled a popular interest in the Huaorani plight.

The Huaorani have chosen an institutional response to the encroachment upon their territory by the arrayed forces of capitalism. The success or failure of such a response is difficult to evaluate, impossible to measure. It is clear that an institutional response such as this requires that the organization be capable of demonstrating power sufficient to be listened to and the ability to operate and negotiate effectively within the political, cultural, and physical space of an alien culture. Whether or not the Huaorani have been able to achieve these goals will not be known for many years.

The demands being made by the newly formed nongovernmental organizations of indigenous peoples are frequently similar. Demands for land–the legalization of large tracts of traditional indigenous territory–head the list (MacDonald 1995b). Education, a voice in national politics, some control over regional development, all become part of a shifting matrix of demands for recognition on the part of indigenous peoples.

Implicit in this institutional/organizational approach to indigenous rights is the necessity of some sort of power and legitimacy with which to confront the government, the capitalists, the military, and the multinational institutions. The act of organization, by itself, does not automatically empower an institution such as ONHAE. Power may come from any of a variety of sources, but without political/economic power an NGO will be without voice. In Ecuador the combined weight of the indigenous organizations, acting through regional and national federations and more recently through the formation of a political party, has given a degree of strength to each of its constituent members. Thus the Huaorani, a numerically small group occupying an extremely valuable tract of land, have been able to command at least the attention of national and international institutions.

Fieldwork

This fieldwork was conducted in 1995 and 1996. I spent the summer of 1995 making contacts with the leaders of ONHAE and their supporters in other organizations. I approached the president of the organization, Armando Boya, with my research proposal, and spent a day explaining to him and to other ONHAE officers exactly what it was that I wished to study. I offered to bring the ONHAE office a computer, on which I would train the leaders, office staff, and any other Huaorani who would be interested. This gave me the access I needed to the day-to-day workings of the organization. I rented and furnished an apartment directly below the office of OPIP/Amazanga in Puyo, and made that apartment a place where Huaorani leaders or those visiting town could drop in or stay. I worked with the leadership of ONHAE in their office in Shell-Mera and accompanied them on frequent visits to Huaorani communities in the forest, as well as to Quito. This permitted me to work alongside the organization's activists on a daily basis. I spent regular business days working in the office, socialized with the leaders in the evening, and frequently hosted the leaders and their relatives in my home in Puyo. I was able to participate directly in the planning of events, and to observe the interactions of the leaders with rank-and-file Huaorani, oil company representatives, environmentalists, tourists, and others. I was the only outside observer at the annual *asemblea* of the organization, and I helped to organize a conference, at the leaders' behest, to discuss the international environmental movement. At the end of my fieldwork I conducted life history interviews with current and former leaders of the organization, as well as leaders of other indigenous organizations who have worked closely (or attempted to work closely) with ONHAE these interviews are quoted extensively throughout this work.

Organization of This Work

The organization of this work is as follows. In Chapter 1, I will provide some background information about the region in which the Huaorani live, including a synthesis of the available geographical, environmental, and historical information based on secondary ethnographic and other works, as well as some of my own observations. The effects of contact with "outsiders" are discussed. The Huaorani have experienced several distinct periods of contact, each of which has been marked by very different consequences. The rubber boom, which swept through the Amazon in the late nineteenth and early twentieth centuries, the beginnings of oil exploration from the 1930s and, most significantly, the penetration of North American evangelical missionaries from the 1960s are discussed. I will focus in particular on this last (and ongoing) penetration of Huaorani territory, examining the political, theological, and personal motivations of the missionaries and missionary organizations. This background provides an introduction to the multiple interpenetrating contexts that both shape and reflect the activities and realities of Huaorani society, and an explication of how they came to be as they were at the time of the foundation of ONHAE.

Chapter 2 provides an account of my fieldwork with ONHAE and begins to point toward some of my conclusions about the organization and its efficacy as well as some of the internal and external relationships that help to place it within its multiple contexts. ONHAE is examined in detail here. The organization's history, its founding, and the struggles of its first years are described, including the flawed but ultimately successful fight for legal recognition of Huaorani territorial rights, and the history of agreements between the organization and the oil companies. The individuals who have led the organization are introduced individually, and generational, cultural, and linguistic characteristics of these principals are described, along with the practices that sustain the organization and the nature of its concrete activities. Finally the organization is placed within the framework of the progressive movements with which it is articulated (however tenuously) and the other interested actors, the balancing of whose various and contradictory influences is central to the activity of ONHAE.

"Power" can come from a myriad of sources. An organization like ONHAE, which does not wield institutionalized power, or power supported by the threat of coercion, depends on the continued acknowledgment of its role and legitimacy both by the Huaorani people and by the non-Huaorani actors it confronts. Chapter 3 looks at the structures and practices that reproduce not just the organization qua institution, but its legitimacy and authority. By examining two events in detail—one involving the organization's internal relationship with the Huaorani people and the other rooted in the relations of ONHAE with the broader Ecuadorian society it is possible to glimpse how the structures developed by the organization have permitted it to maintain its apparent legitimacy in representing the Huaorani people. The first part of the chapter is an account of the *Biye,* or annual assembly, of ONHAE in 1996, which I was privileged to attend. The *Biye,* a gathering of Huaorani from all of the scattered communities, is the prime source of ONHAE's legitimacy within Huaorani society and the group's highest governing body. Part two of the chapter examines the Huaorani participation in the annual 12 May parade in Puyo, where Huaorani representations of themselves in a cross-cultural context are juxtaposed with the very different participation and behavior of the ONHAE leadership.

Chapter 4 looks at the goals, successes and failures of ONHAE and attempts to provide the beginnings of an evaluation of the organization's work. The chapter reviews the stated goals of the organization over time, and examines the compromises that have been made. The relationships of power and persuasion that exist between ONHAE and the oil companies, missionaries, environmental movement, and the state are explored. These elements have generated new challenges to Huaorani culture and society, fostering changes in gender relations and roles, community identity, and pan-Huaorani consciousness, all of which have been reflected in the organization's actions.

Finally, I present my conclusions about ONHAE and begin what I hope will be a continuing process of looking for ways in which the experience of ONHAE can provide practical lessons for future generations of Huaorani leaders, as well as other indigenous organizations. The central theses of this work are explored once again, and the relationship and importance of this study to anthropology and anthropological theory are discussed.

Notes

1. *Oriente* is the term applied throughout Ecuador to refer to the country's Amazonian territory.
2. CONFENIAE is the Confederación de las Nacionalidades Indígenas de la Amazonia Ecuatoriana and CONAIE is the Confederación de Nacionalidades Indígenas del Ecuador.
3. Notably Laura Rival, whose fieldwork in Quehueire Ono was underway at the time of ONHAE's founding.
4. Among the many examples of this sort of attention are the activities of the rock star Sting, reports on the Huaorani by NBC television's "Dateline" program (1994), the popularity of Joe Kane's 1995 book on the Huaorani, and the exhibit "Mysteries of the Amazon" at the Philadelphia Academy of Natural Sciences (2000).

Chapter 1

HISTORY AND BACKGROUND

The Huaorani cannot be discussed without an understanding of the multiple contexts of their environment. The origins of the Huaorani people and the roots of their culture are unrecorded. Much of the history that we do have is the story of contacts between the Huaorani people and non-Huaorani. Each of these contacts must be understood as collisions which have shaped the trajectory of Huaorani cultural development—a dialectical process of crisis, reaction, and resolution.

Beyond the natural environment—itself a key factor in the development of Huaorani social organization—the twentieth century evolution of Huaorani cultural practice has taken place within a context of increasing encroachment on Huaorani land and cultural practices by outsiders. The principal actors in this conflicted space are the rubber merchants and slave dealers of the early part of the century, and more recently the evangelical missionaries, oil companies, and expanding indigenous neighbors of the Huaorani. This chapter provides an introduction to the environmental and historical contexts of the Huaorani. Their culture has evolved in a very particular ecological niche, so a discussion of the geography and ecology of the region is needed. Further, the extent of the Huaorani isolation from the rest of the world will be described. The Huaorani have usually been por-

Notes for this section can be found on page 74.

trayed–implicitly or explicitly – in published accounts as living in "isolation," apart from all others (see Broenniman 1981; Elliot 1981; Wallis 1960; and discussion in Rival 1994: 253-88). In fact, this has suited the needs of certain groups of people who have wished to exoticize and use the Huaorani in one way or another. The missionaries raise money through their tales of isolated "savage tribes" in the Amazon; further, their own sense of what they are doing is based on "reaching the most remote corners of the world with the word of God" (Saint 1996). People interested in seeing themselves as "adventurers" objectified the Huaorani as "primitive" in order to form the proper backdrop for their own feats of daring (Broenniman 1981; Kane 1995). As discussed by Rival (1994), the Ecuadorian media has also frequently portrayed the Huaorani as exotic savages. In the Ecuadorian national consciousness the "Auca"[1] represent a wild, fearful, and dangerous "other"–in a sense, the wild side of the national character. Alternatively (and simultaneously), however, the national media has identified them as representative of the "noble savage"–an exotic, wise tribe of spiritual and mysterious people who live in perfect harmony with their surroundings. This idealist view has also permeated much of the discourse being generated by the international environmental movement, in which the Huaorani are depicted as helpless innocents whose well developed environmental consciousness is juxtaposed against the rapacity of multinational corporations and the venality of the government of Ecuador. The truth of course, is that the Huaorani are not truly "isolated," for they exist within a variety of local, national, regional, and global political and social contexts and always have. Even before pacific contact took place, their hostility, fear, and avoidance of "outsiders" (*cowode*) were defining factors in the development of their society. The Huaorani may certainly be viewed as *different* from others, but they cannot be viewed in isolation or without reference to the social, political, and environmental contexts of their society.

Geography

Strictly speaking, the Amazon Basin is a riverine drainage area extending from the continental divide of the Andean chain in the west and northwest, to the Atlantic Ocean in the east, and from what is today north central Brazil to the beginning of the Río Platte drainage in the Matto Grosso and Chaco forests. In practice, however, it is more useful to think of the "Amazon Basin" as an area that encompasses all of the tropical forest regions from the Andes to northern Argentina, thus including the Orinoco Basin, all of the Chaco, and the forests of the Guyanas. The Amazon represents one of the largest and most diverse regional ecosystems in the world. This diversity extends to biological, geological, and cultural variance. The region contains more species of plants and animals (many still unclassified by western science) than any other. Historically, it seems likely to have constituted a "refuge zone" during the last ice age–that is, one of the areas in which older species were able to survive the period of dramatic climatic change. Homo sapiens is a relatively recent addition to this diversity, arriving within the last 10,000 years. In this brief period, a wide variety of cultural/ethnic groups have formed; more than twelve of Julian Steward's twenty-two "culture areas" are located at least partly within the region (Murdock 1974; Steward and Faron 1959). Although perhaps useful taxonomic structures, the reality of Amazonian cultures is much more complex than Steward's areas would indicate. A quick look at some of the other attempts at classification (Lowie 1961; Sorenson 1967; Meggers 1996) demonstrates that linguistic and other evidence indicates much more fragmented and multivariate origins for Amazonian groups.

The Ecuadorian piece of the Amazon drainage basin is part of the westernmost rim of the region, beginning at the continental divide and running east to the (disputed) Peruvian border. Several elements distinguish the Ecuadorian Amazon: its altitude, the presence of an array of distinct microclimates, and (not unrelated to the previous point) the presence of a great diversity of indigenous groups.

As one enters the region, particularly by air, one is struck by the rugged, mountainous topography. Most of the Amazon is relatively flat–hence the meandering flow of such great quantities of water. But in Ecuador the region drops dramatically, from over 4,000 meters (with intermittent peaks of more than 5,000) to below 600 meters near the Peruvian border, therefore leaving only 600 meters of "fall" from Ecuador to the Atlantic Ocean. What this cre-

ates in Ecuador is a seemingly endless variety of "microclimates."
Within each band of altitude, there exist distinct climatic zones,
delineated and physically separated by the mountain ridges that
spread out like fingers along the basin. These formations contain
species of flora and fauna which are in many cases unique to the
particular microclimate. There are surprising disparities as well in
the amount of rainfall received, seasonality of the rain (how distinct
the "rainy season" is in a particular area), and temperature. The
ruggedness of the terrain and other difficulties hindering movement from one to another of these areas have provided a degree of
isolation to the indigenous groups that reside there.

People

The diversity mentioned above is manifest in the wide variety of
quite different ethnic groups to be found in the Ecuadorian Amazon. The time depth of this diversity is evident in the linguistic, economic, and organizational differences that exist between relatively
small groups occupying geographically close, even neighboring
territories. The Huaorani, in particular, have been referred to by
James Yost (1981a: 677) as a linguistic isolate whose language is
unrelated to those of neighboring groups, and Rival (1992: 55), cit-
ing Whitten, states that Huao Terero (the Huaorani language) is
notable for its extremely small number of "borrowed" words. The
social organization of production varies markedly among, for
example, the Shuar, Quijos (lowland) Quichua, and Huaorani
groups, although it is difficult to arrive at an accurate picture of
their pre-Columbian economic structures relying on only the
accounts of the early Jesuit missionaries in the area. Among the
groups identified by Linda Newson (1995: 83-105) as inhabiting the
Ecuadorian *oriente* in pre-Columbian times are the Cofán, Coron-
ado, Quijos, Macas, Zaparoan, Panoan, Kandoshi, Jívaro [sic],
Omagua, and Tucanoan peoples. Many of these groups did not
long survive the Spanish conquest, and either died off completely
or assimilated within other indigenous groups. The tragic result has
been labeled "ethnic simplification" (Muratorio 1991: 40-43)–a
time in which circumstances (disease, *reducciones*, etc.) brought

about a decrease in the diversity or led to the homogenization of the ethnic groups in the region.

The critical phase in the modern development of the Ecuadorian Amazon was the rubber boom. The effects of this boom on the Huaorani specifically will be discussed in more detail below; here I wish to provide a general overview of the boom and its effects on the structures of economic life in the region generally. In 1839 Goodyear discovered a process to vulcanize natural rubber–the product of a tree that only grows wild in the Amazon. By the 1880s enormous demand for rubber from European and North American industrial capitalists had led to a rubber boom throughout all of the Amazon basin. A thorough discussion of the effects of the rubber boom in the Ecuadorian Amazon would merit a full book-length treatment, but here it is enough to cover some basic facts that must be considered when we speak of the experiences of the local indigenous populations. First, traders, merchants, and middlemen, who were engaged in a fierce competition as much for workers as for rubber itself, resorted to the widespread use of slavery and other forms of coercive labor. Later, as the conditions of the boom became unstable and the lower-quality rubber of the Ecuadorian Amazon failed to maintain its high price, rubber merchants became slave merchants, selling large numbers of Amazonian indigenous people in slave markets as far away as Iquitos and Manaus in order to satisfy their debts (Muratorio 1991: 104-6). Late in the nineteenth century the British smuggled rubber tree seeds out of Brazil and successfully grew them in their colonies in southern Asia, which effectively and abruptly ended the rubber boom in South America. It should be noted that as devastating as the impact of the rubber boom was for Amazonian indigenous populations, and as profound as were the social changes it wrought in the region, it did not have the same national consequences that other bursts of growth had. The nineteenth-century cacao boom, for example, established the lasting primacy of an agricultural bourgeoisie from the Pacific coastal provinces, while the late twentieth-century oil boom has led to the penetration of international extractive capitalism and a new experience of foreign domination, neocolonialism, and debt peonage.

Muratorio (1991: 106-7) identifies the rubber boom as the time of the first really significant capitalist penetration of the Ecuadorian

Amazon and calls the rubber merchants "intermediaries for the penetration of industrial capitalism into the Amazon," but I would qualify this statement: I believe that the rubber boom was not a penetration *by* capitalism but a penetration by precapitalist or what I call "paracapitalist" forces launched by the capitalist enterprises of the time. It is true that the end users of the material produced (rubber) were capitalists, and to some extent it may be argued that the traders who acted as middlemen between the collectors and the agents of foreign capital represented some sort of incipient mercantile or *comprador* bourgeoisie, but the collectors and the organization of production did not represent immanent capitalism. On the contrary, the widespread use of actual slavery, threats, torture, and terror on the part of the rubber merchants is more consistent with precapitalist economic organization. Further, no attempt was made to rationalize or expand production—virtually all South American rubber production during the boom was based on the gathering of wild rubber.

The Huaorani

Any attempt to provide an account of the origins of the Huaorani or of their history prior to the twentieth century is speculative. Cabodevilla (1994) has attempted such an account, relying on references found in accounts of other neighboring groups, and Whitten (quoted in Rival: 1992, 55-6) has found evidence to indicate the ancestors of the Huaorani were Zaparoan refugees. What is clear is that the Huaorani existed in more or less their current territory by the time of the rubber boom in the late nineteenth and early twentieth centuries, and that they may have been in contact with one or more of the eighteenth-century Jesuit mission stations in the area.

    One reason for the astounding cultural diversity of the *oriente* is that the Ecuadorian Amazon was never conquered by any of the great tributary states of the pre-Columbian Andes. Chavin and the other pre-Inca states never expanded eastward to any great extent. Only the late Inca Empire ever effectively penetrated the territory that makes up modern Ecuador, and this conquest was confined to the sierra. Although the Inca Empire had penetrated far to the east of the continental divide in southern Peru, they never had the opportunity to similarly expand into the Ecuadorian Amazon, although they did enter the region on at least several occasions. It is also worth noting that Quichua (the northern variant of the Inca/ Peruvian Quechua) was well established as the lingua franca of the upper Amazon before the arrival of the Spanish. It has been suggested (Urban and Sherzer 1988; Urban 1991) that Quichua had already established itself before the Inca conquest took place, possibly as early as 800 C.E.. Clearly, it was in the interests of efficient colonial administration and the most orderly exploitation of the indigenous societies that the Spaniards encourage the spread of a single language. Thus Quichua became the generally used language of Ecuador's upper Amazon, where Spanish colonial administration was firmly established quite early.

Farther to the east, however, where difficulties in transport and communication made the efficient establishment of Spanish rule more problematic, active and open resistance to the Spanish was more common. In the sixteenth century the Jesuits established a series of missions, accompanied by the creation of *encomiendas* (part of a system of plantation agriculture based on essentially feudal labor relationships, with indigenous people tied as serfs to particular *encomenderos*) and *reducciones* (reservations). This led to at least one massive, multi-ethnic rebellion against Spanish (and particularly Jesuit) rule in 1578-79. This rebellion was brutally suppressed and followed by punitive expeditions in which the Spanish hunted indigenous people in order to quarter them. Following the rebellion, the only effective resistance open to the indigenous populations was to escape the jurisdiction of the *encomenderos* by falling back deeper into the forest. Additionally, while living within the social contexts of these colonial institutions, members of different indigenous groups were forced to live side by side. At the same time, new diseases (particularly smallpox and measles) brought by the Spanish led to further massive decreases in population. The result has been labeled "ethnic simplification" (Muratorio 1991)–a time in which circumstances brought about a decrease in diversity or the homogenization of the ethnic groups in the region.

In 1767 the Jesuits were expelled from the region, and the indigenous people were left in the hands of a small and dwindling

number of Spanish settlers and adventurers. In 1830 Ecuador
became independent of Spain. Throughout the early years of the
republic, the upper reaches of the *oriente* were subjected periodically
to harsh attempts by the Quiteño governments to institute one new
policy or another and otherwise to general neglect and widespread
corruption, abuse, and violence–in one period the government
actually ceded control over its eastern provinces to the Jesuits after
they were readmitted in the mid nineteenth century. In the end, during the 1890s, a dispute that developed between the Jesuits and the
trading bourgeoisie led first to open rebellion beginning in 1892
and then to the victory of the traders (now linked with the trade in
rubber) and a change in the nature of Ecuadorian Amazonian society; in time, this new local dominant class would be the default
power in even the Huaorani territory. In the lower *oriente*, virtually
no attempt was made to enforce any but the most nominal administration of the region. Thus the various indigenous peoples of the
lower *oriente* (including what is today the territory of the Huaorani)
experienced a period of what was, for them, benign neglect.

     None of the early missionary or explorer accounts concerning
the indigenous peoples of the region have been found to make any
explicit reference to the "Huaorani." Different contemporary writers have attempted to glean information about the ancestors of the
Huao people from references to groups that have seemed to share
cultural or territorial traits with the Huaorani.

     Cabodevilla (1994) has attempted a history of the Huaorani
that places the Huao people in contact with Catholic missionaries
and explorers as early as 1592. These accounts refer to the Omaguas, a warlike group living near present-day Huaorani territory.
Cabodevilla's highly speculative account relies on sketchy and
obscure chronicles left by early Jesuit missionaries, containing little
information that would confirm that these people were indeed the
Huaorani. Bertha Fuentes (1997: 79-81) has reviewed summaries of
the old missionary records of the period from 1538 to 1669 and has
found that within the "Zaparo block" there were groups referred to
variously as Omaguas, Abijiras, Aushiris, and Agouis. Whitten
(quoted in Rival 1992: 55) also indicates that the ancestors of the
Huaorani were Zaparoan. True, the Zaparo were riverine people,
while the Huao specialize in the "hinterland" or highland areas;

this may however represent a refugee strategy adopted by some Zaparoan groups–attempting to get away from the relatively high visibility of the river's edge. The missionary accounts refer to inter-tribal conflict and warfare that created refugee populations and affected migration patterns. Fuentes identifies these displaced groups as "proto-Huaorani" and claims that they represent the northernmost extension of the migrations of Tupi-guaraní, also identified as Omaguas. Fuentes goes on to describe how in 1605 and again in 1620 Rafael Ferrer organized expeditions on the Rio Napo and found that the "Abijiris" inhabited the southern banks of the Napo. There are accounts that indicate that after resisting mis-sionization and the *encomenderos*, they were finally subjugated in 1620-21 but soon rebelled, fleeing to the southern bank of the Napo (present-day Huaorani territory).

The Franciscan priest Father Laureano de la Cruz who com-piled data on the indigenous people of the region in 1636, described people ("Aubixiris") living on the south bank of the Napo (the heart of present-day Huaorani territory). His description sounds plausibly similar to the Huaorani:

> The province of the Aubixiri indians, where we had to enter, is on the great Rio Napo, on the right hand side going down, which is the south bank and has its beginnings in the same parange as the Encabellados, and the populations continue for more than fifty leagues; they say it is a very heavily populated area. All of these lands are hilly and very forested where they have their houses, which are two or three leagues distant from the river, where it is all forest. Their houses are divided into villages of from four to six, to eight houses and each one has one or two indian men, their women, and their children. The hamlets are separated from each other by a quarter league, a half league or a league. The houses are made of wood and covered with palm, and are all open. The indians all go around naked, they sleep in hammocks and they sustain themselves with corn [maize] which they gather in abundance, and by yucca [manioc] which are roots that they plant, they also have much cassava, and chontarura which is a palm fruit that they cultivate; and these types and other similar is what serves in this country for food and drink. They have honey from bees, which they raise in the holes in trees, although they do not use the wax. They have much fish, wild game, and wild fruits. They have much tobacco which they all use and inhale the smoke. These lands hold promise if they are cultivated for other purposes like rice, cacao, sweet [sugar?] cane and good cotton (Compte 1885: 157-58).

Information about this region of Amazonia is characterized by contradictory statements, lack of certainty about the identity of specific ethnic groups, and self-serving and racist depictions of the indigenous peoples of the area. Nevertheless, certain statements about the Huaorani past can be made with some degree of certainty, and although information specifically about the Huaorani may be scarce in these early records, it is reasonable to assume that changes occurring in the vicinity of the Huaorani had to have affected the developmental trajectory of their society. We know that large numbers of other indigenous peoples fled into the forest in fear of the *encomenderos*, and it is certainly logical to suppose that if the Huaorani were already inhabiting approximately their current territory by this time, they were aware of what was going on and probably fearful of the Christian outsiders.

Further, we know that new diseases were brought into the area, and although the Huaorani people seem to have avoided at least some of these epidemics,[2] they were certainly affected by the tremendous reductions in population that took place as a result, freeing great areas of land and possibly facilitating the Huaorani practices of geographic dispersal and seminomadism (Newson 1995: 325-48).

The rubber boom was the first in a series of cataclysmic events in the recent development of Huao culture. Some Huaorani were forced to work on the rubber haciendas, their villages were raided and their children seized and sold in the slave markets of Iquitos, many were killed outright, and many more died as a result of exposure to new diseases (Cabodevilla 1994: 135-54; CONAIE 1989: 73; Rival 1992: 55-59; Robarchek and Robarchek 1998: 89-90; Smith 1993: 10-13). Other indigenous groups (Shuar, Zaparo, etc.) raided their territory, and also entered it as rubber workers (Muratorio 1991: 102-9, 134-6). At least one instance of an attack by the Huaorani on a rubber hacienda has been documented (Dall'Alba 1992: 14-19; Smith 1993: 10-11). While it is only possible to speculate on the characteristics of pre-rubber boom Huao society, it is evident that the Huaorani hostility toward outsiders was (at least partly) a result of this disastrous episode of contact.

General Characteristics of "Traditional" Huao Culture

In some ways it is difficult to provide even the most basic description of Huaorani cultural practices. Because of the rapidity and character of the changes that have taken place in Huao society in the last twenty to thirty years, it is increasingly difficult to know what traditional Huao practices really were–James Yost, the first anthropologist to work extensively with the Huaorani, has never produced a general ethnographic study for publication. Later writers, including Rival (1992), Fuentes (1997), and Clayton and Carole Robarchek (1998), have provided some ethnographic information, but in just the few years since their work was done substantial changes have swept Huaorani society. Thus I am frequently unable to "see" what they witnessed, not because of inaccuracy on their part but because practices have shifted. Getting the information from the Huaorani themselves is equally problematic because it is clear that their own recounting of the past is colored by the present; Huaorani informants consistently placed a great deal of emphasis on the past, but changed stories of the past to suit present needs or desires. Nevertheless, I can undertake to present some of the most basic information based on my own observations compared with the work of Yost, Rival, and the Robarcheks.

A further observation about Huaorani behavior and social organization is important here. Despite some of the descriptions of rigid rules governing such things as sexual division of labor, food taboos, and appropriate marriage partners that one may find in the works of such anthropologists as Napoleon Chagnon, Jacques Lizot, Robert Lowie, and others, Huaorani society is typified more than anything by a relaxed and pragmatic view of their own norms and rules. This has been noted by most social scientists and observers who have worked among them including Smith (1996–personal communication), Rival (1992), Yost (1981a: 690-98), and Robarchek and Robarchek (1998: 57 and 102-5). For any rule there will be many exceptions. It was not possible for me to locate a single *nanicabo* (extended family or "longhouse group") that fit exactly the description of the "proper membership" for such an entity. Huaorani culture is always being negotiated and is sufficiently flexible to adapt itself quickly to changing conditions and influences.

Traditionally, the Huaorani are hunter/gatherer/horticulturists. In the rain forests of the eastern slope of the Andes, their diet consists of meat obtained by hunting (primarily howler and spider monkeys, peccary, jungle deer, and a variety of birds) and manioc (*yuca*) grown in their gardens, which is made into a mild fermented drink called *tepe* by the Huaorani and *chicha* in both Quichua and in Ecuadorian Spanish (unlike the *chicha* drunk by most Amazonian groups, the *tepe* of the Huaorani generally has only a negligible alcohol content). It is *tepe* that provides the bulk of the calories in the Huaorani diet, being its most reliable element, but meat is the most prized and sought-after foodstuff.

In addition, the Huaorani gather a variety of fruits and other foods from the forest, most notably the peach palm fruit (*chonta*), which is in season from about mid February to April or May. Rival (1998: 635-52) has completed a detailed study of the importance of these trees in Huao society and has found that the trees are not wild, and in fact are not capable of self-propagation without human intervention. All of the individual trees are "owned" by particular *nanicabos* (extended family economic units, discussed below), which retain hereditary rights to the fruit. Elizabeth Conklin (1999) has said that "space in the Amazon is saturated with the residue of human agency" and it is true that all of the forests surrounding the Huaorani are, in effect, "managed" forests, where trees are cut, new plants and trees are encouraged over others, and trails and river crossings are maintained.

An unusual and important aspect of Huao society is that before the initiation of pacific contact with non-Huaorani, they lived not at the banks of the larger rivers, as is the case with most Amazonian hunter-gatherer groups, but on the tops of the interfluvial ridges that rise sharply from the banks of rivers. Until the 1950s the Huaorani had no knowledge of canoe making and did not know how to swim. This is still reported to be true of the Tagaeri and Taromenga groups, which have continued to violently resist contact with the "outside" – in this case including other groups of Huaorani. At least on the surface, it seems probable that this is in part a refugee strategy: by inhabiting the high ridges and avoiding the navigable waterways the Huao were able to avoid most contact with the non-Huaorani who frequently traverse the rivers, and by placing themselves on the high ground they were also in a better defensive position in the event of attack. Yost (1981a: 682-85) presents evidence to indicate that this residential pattern has considerable time depth.

The economic and social units of most importance are the *nanicabos*–residential units generally made up of extended families, but not infrequently including distant kin and others (refugees from attacks, for example). According to both Rival (1992: 108-16) and my informants, the rules for membership in the *nanicabos* were at one time in the distant past much more rigidly defined. Following periods of frequent raiding and warfare, and the imposition of missionary contact (1957 to the present), the rules regarding membership (as well as the rules for appropriate marriage partners, as will be discussed below) have become much more fluid and adaptable.

In the past, the *nanicabo* was a physical entity, essentially a "longhouse group." Over the last thirty years this has become somewhat less true, particularly in those communities within the boundaries of the protectorate that have come under the strongest missionary influence (Toñampade, Tiweno, Tzapino). In these communities the *nanicabo* is frequently a group of separate houses accommodating western-style "nuclear families," which are the constituent parts of the nanicabo membership; these families constantly visit one another, women will go to their shared gardens together, and food and other goods as well as work are shared between them. The missionaries, and in particular Rachel Saint, have long indicated their contempt for communal living. Their encouragement of the Huaorani to build separate houses for each married couple and their children has been instrumental in the destruction of this core component of Huao social life. Earlier, there might have been up to a mile of space between the *nanicabos* that made up a more traditional "village," and some groups chose to live in isolated settlements consisting of only one *nanicabo*. Today, most Huao villages have a school, and the majority have an airstrip as well, which means that households are established closer together in order to gain proximity to these institutions.

Although there are probably more exceptions than there are cases that strictly adhere to all of these rules, the "ideal" *nanicabo* includes one or two male heads of household, usually brothers and their wives, unmarried children, daughters, and sons-in-law. Since the preferred marriage partner is always one's cross-cousin (the children of ego's father's sisters or ego's mother's brothers), and since a large portion of eligible marriage partners will normally be members of the same *nanicabo* (and therefore prohibited as potential mates), endogamous marriage is frequent. Today the customs regarding marriage eligibility seem to be eroding, and significant numbers of Huaorani have married outside of their cross-cousins and some have even married non-Huaorani. Such marriages, usually between Quichua men and Huaorani women are often criticized by Huaorani, who claim that the Quichua want to marry a Huaorani woman only to gain access to the comparatively pristine hunting territories of the Huaorani territory. However, the cross cousin rules are still used to determine sexual access; ordinarily (before missionization) a man may have sex with his spouse's siblings and his sibling's spouses. In my observations this sexual contact was entirely heterosexual, although men are generally very physical with each other; but Robarchek and Robarchek (1998: 56-57, 106, and 138) and Smith (1996, personal communication) have indicated that homosexual encounters (at least among males) are also common. Clayton and Carol Robarchek also provide a reasonable explanation for this being hidden from western researchers–after more than forty years of contact with fundamentalist Christian missionaries, mostly from the southern or midwestern United States, they know well enough how to hide what will certainly be disapproved of.

The *nanicabo* is the primary unit in the social organization of production. Food, which is obtained by any member of the *nanicabo,* must be apportioned to all members of the household before any is given to members of other households. Hunting parties generally begin in a single *nanicabo,* although others frequently join the group as it leaves, particularly in the more geographically compact villages built around the nexus of a school, airstrip, and radio. Within the *nanicabo* chores are jointly undertaken, and all food and material goods are shared. There is a sexual division of labor, in which men take the primary responsibility for hunting while women take primary responsibility for gardening, gathering from the forest, cooking, and child care; however, among the Huaorani all of these lines are fluid and flexible (Robarchek and Robarchek

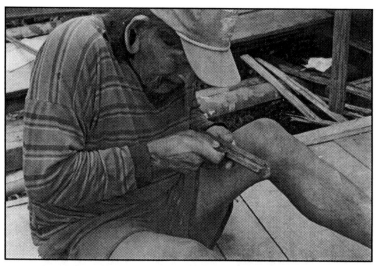

The shaman Mengotohue manufacturing a blowgun.

Yasuní. A woman prepares blowgun darts.

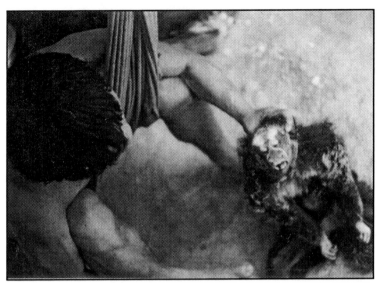

A Huaorani hunter shows off a woolly monkey.

Woman of the Yasuní group prepares tepe.

Quehueire Ono. Parent teacher meeting at the village school.

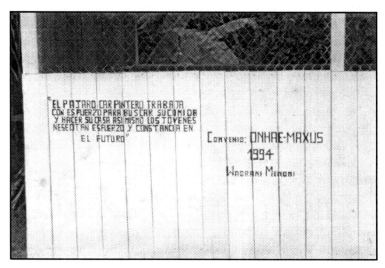

Toñampade. School built by Maxus.

1998: 104-6; Yost 1981b: 109). I have seen men of all ages routinely participate in child care, work in the gardens, and gather plants and insects from the forest. I have also seen women hunt, usually under one of three types of circumstance: first, opportunistic hunting–something has wandered into or near the community or garden, and the woman kills it, usually with her machete; second, as part of a hunt involving the entire *nanicabo*, particularly when large concentrations of an animal are moving near the community; and finally, when the woman's husband is away working for "*la compañia*" (any one of the many oil production companies or consortiums operating in Huaorani territory). Fishing, which, as discussed earlier, was not a part of traditional (pre-contact) Huaorani society, is now common and is routinely done by both men and women. The only activity I have never seen men do while in the household is cooking, although I have seen men serve themselves (and very occasionally guests) from pots of leftovers. Women and girls are the primary weavers of hammocks, string bags, and other textiles; while men are primarily responsible for the production of spears and blowguns, as well as the arduous task of canoe manufacture–but again, in each of these cases, there is little rigidity in these sex roles, and I have seen men weave and women participate in woodworking (particularly in the long process of hollowing out a canoe).

As noted as well by Rival (1992: 116), Robarchek and Robarchek (1998: 57), Yost (1995, personal communication), and Smith (1996, personal communication), Huaorani domestic relations are notable in the Amazon region for their peaceful and cooperative nature. In fact, I can reiterate the observations of Rival and Robarchek and Robarchek–I have not only never witnessed domestic violence of any kind, but my informants have been unable (or unwilling) to name a single instance of such behavior. Andy Drumm, a social scientist and environmentalist who has worked with the Huaorani for more than a decade, states (1999, personal communication) that he has witnessed one occasion when a Huao husband (who had been working away from the community with the oil companies) beat up his wife in Quehueire Ono, and he adds that the rest of the community was disapproving and shocked by the behavior. Huaorani men help with domestic tasks and decision making, both within the *nanicabo* and at the *Biye* (the annual "*con-*

greso" of ONHAE), and at school and village meetings both women and men contribute to the discussion.

Prior to ONHAE and missionization there was no pan-Huaorani consciousness. The Huaorani all share the same language (Huao Terero), which is not spoken by any other group. But there were no ritual societies, "tribal" organizations or leadership, no age sets between different *nanicabos* – in short, nothing that might have represented a sense of group identity as "Huaorani."

Huaorani Decision Making

Decision making processes in traditional Huaorani society seem to have been built on consensus. Groups were small (in 1958 there were fewer than 600 Huaorani inhabiting a territory roughly equivalent in size to the island of Puerto Rico), and where consensus became impossible villages and/or *nanicabos* would "fission" and relocate (for a description of similar settlement patterns among the Yanomamö, see Chagnon 1992: 76-77). At times, such failures to resolve disputes have resulted in violence, including spearing raids and cycles of vengeance (Robarchek and Robarchek 1998: 24-26; Yost 1981b: 110-11). Although little has been written specifically on the topic, it seems that before pacific contact began in the 1950s, there were few formal structures for decision making.

In discussing decision making I will use the word *power* to signify the ability to compel obedience or acquiescence, and I will use the word *authority* to indicate something very different–the ability to wield influence to a greater degree than some others. In this context the Huaorani have no formally recognized leaders, and no individual has any greater *power* than anyone else does. Some individuals are somewhat more influential than others, including shamans and older people ("los guerreros ancianos"); however, these individuals participate alongside the other members of the community in the process of discussion and consensus building and do not give commands or in any way make unilateral decisions for the group. Robarchek and Robarchek (1998: 123) confirm that the Huaorani are without distinctions of rank. Today, owing to the influence of non-Huaorani in the creation of formalized social institutions, the Huaorani are accustomed to more formal meetings, at which order (of some sort) is maintained by someone. This takes place in the schools, where parent-teacher meetings are attended by whole villages, in the churches of the more missionary-dominated settlements, and at organizational meetings called by the Huaorani themselves, most particularly the *Biye*. These more formal meetings were specifically introduced by the Protestant missionaries, who also introduced western notions of "voting" and "majority rule." While the Huaorani have now incorporated formal meetings into their group decision making repertory, they still have largely retained the goal of consensus in place of voting and majority decision making, except in certain specific instances.

Meetings that take place in the schools are run by teachers who, as will be discussed in detail in the next chapter, are almost exclusively non-Huaorani (they may be Quichua, Shuar, mestizo, or North American), so although the Huaorani are participants in the meetings, they are still largely an activity imposed and conducted by non-Huaorani agents. Meetings connected with village churches, where they exist, are now generally run by the Huaorani, but those Huaorani who have become active church members are generally the most completely westernized, acculturated, and nontraditional. These individuals are actively seeking to emulate the behavior and forms of the North American missionaries.

The *Biye*, however, is an example of the incorporation of an imposed cultural practice (large formal meetings) within a very traditional sensibility and the creation of supporting ideological devices to ground the practice neatly within the long established patterns of Huao culture. The *Biye* (or "*congreso*," as it is called in Spanish), which is the annual meeting of ONHAE, will be discussed in detail in Chapter 4. It is a remarkably open and democratic process in which any Huaorani attending may raise any issue for discussion. Only at the end of the three – or four – day process are there any formal votes, and these represent the approval process for what I can best describe as a "sense of the meeting" resolution and votes held for the election of officers. The Huaorani leadership claim that the *Biye* is a traditional method of resolving disputes between villages or *nanicabos* and that it has always not only existed, but taken place in what is more or less its current form. However, when older Huaorani were asked to describe the traditional *Biye*, not one of them remembered one taking place, let alone having attended any. Although I was unable to pin down the origins of the word, it seems that while there may have been some sort of meeting between different *nanicabos* in the past, it was neither common nor formalized. At the *Biye*, discussion of each issue goes on until an unspoken consensus is reached; the closest thing I can compare it to is a meeting for business of the Society of Friends (Quakers). Men and women both actively participate in the discussions (as well as the votes that take place at the closing of the meeting). In their discussions with me ONHAE leaders, former leaders, and *Biye* attendees all stated that gender was not an issue for the Huaorani, that everyone was "equal" at the meeting, and that anyone could speak; in practice, however, I observed that the ceremonial "chair" of the meeting was invariably a male (Juan Huamoni, Mengotuhue, Armando Boya). Furthermore, only one woman was an elected official and she, Nancy, was vice president for health and education–traditionally areas of women's concern. Additionally, she was the daughter of Dayuma (arguably the most powerful individual Huaorani) and the wife of a prominent Quichua educator. Until the end of the *Biye* no one tried to restate the "sense of the meeting," but at the closing of the *Biye* the president of ONHAE presented a written statement (in Spanish as well as *Huao Terero*) of the resolutions of the *Biye* that was discussed, debated, edited, and finally approved by the attendees.

Warfare, Spear Killing, and Violence

Largely as a result of the efforts of missionary propaganda, the Ecuadorian press, and land-hungry neighboring groups, the name Huaorani has become synonymous with violence, spear killing, and hostility to outsiders. Clearly too, it is true the pre-contact Huaorani were in a state of more or less constant warfare both with "outsiders" (*cowode*–cannibals or non-humans) and with more distantly related *Huao Terero* speaking people living in other clusters of *nanicabos* (*huarani*–other people). Perhaps because of this reputation, warfare and spear killing have been the most studied aspects of Huao society (Kane 1993, 1995; Rival 1992; Robarchek & Robarchek 1998; Yost 1981a, 1981b, and others). It is not my intention to present a thorough exploration of spear killing or its role in Huaorani life and history, but it is an important aspect of how the Huaorani see themselves. When I was given my name and made a part of a *nanicabo*, the first thing that the older males wanted to show me and teach me was the correct use of a spear. When the Huaorani leaders became frustrated with the machinations of "la compañia" or anyone else, they inevitably referred to the use of violence–and more specifically spears–to enforce compliance or exact revenge. Of course, they are aware of the impracticality of the idea of using force against vast multinational enterprises, but their choice of rhetoric reveals a great deal about the importance that is still placed on spear killing. There are also those who claim that spear killing is a thing of the past, something that belongs with the historic Huaorani tradition of stretched earlobes, but the truth is that spear killing is still something that happens, albeit less frequently than before, throughout the territory. In 1973 a Texaco oil drilling crew was killed by a group of Huaorani; in 1987 the Tagaeri killed Monsignor Alejandro LaBaca and a woman; in November of 1995 a group from Quehueire Ono raided the ranch of a group of Shuar colonists, killing everyone (I visited the site of this raid a few months later); and in July of 1996 I witnessed a raiding party leaving to (at least) confront a group of mestizo "*colonos*" near Tzapino. What does seem to have changed is that warfare among Huaorani has ended, at least for all practical purposes, which means that the cycle of vengeance killings has been broken. Yost (1981a: 695-96), himself affiliated with the missionaries, attributes the end of the cycle of vengeance killing to the teachings of the missionaries and views the role of the church service itself more as the weekly renewal of a pacific social contract than a specific expression of Christian beliefs.

According to Yost (1981b: 101; 1981a: 687), who was the first anthropologist to work extensively with the Huaorani and who began by collecting genealogies and life histories for each Huao household, in the period immediately preceding contact 41 percent of all deaths were attributable to one Huaorani killing another. A further 8 percent of all deaths were attributable to killings carried out by "*cowode*"–usually either Quichua neighbors or slave hunters seeking rubber workers. And another 7 percent of "deaths" (as described by the Huaorani) were attributable to Huaorani being stolen or captured by outsiders. It is important to note, however, that several of the generations surveyed by Yost were dramatically affected by a dramatic example of deviance; sometime in the 1940s a raid took place that killed the parents of an individual named Moipa, who then appears to have become unbalanced and begun a killing and raiding spree accompanied by tremendous violence. As Robarchek and Robarchek put it, Moipa "apparently enjoyed killing for its own sake" (1998: 26). This constant activity, perpetrated in the face of Huaorani concepts of blood vengeance, led to a period in which raids and spear killings resulted in a steady decrease in the population. Because this immediately preceded the arrival of the North American missionaries the picture they compiled of Huao life , given the small Huao population at the time, was distorted. But the truth is that we do not and cannot know just how frequent warfare cycles were in normal pre-contact Huaorani society.

Randy Smith, an environmental activist and observer of the Huaorani, conducted a census of each of the Huaorani communities (not including the still uncontacted Tagaeri and Taromenga groups) that was published in 1993. This count, which I have found to be fairly accurate for the communities included, indicates a total Huaorani population at the time of 1,282. The largest community, according to Smith, is the missionary center of Toñampade with a population of 223, followed by Quehueire Ono with 212 and Quihuaro with 139. The rest of the population live in fifteen additional communities scattered throughout the territory that range in size from 6 (Acaro, inside the former Protectorate) to 82 (Tihueno, the older of the missionary settlements). According to Smith, eleven of these communities have schools, and another 11, not necessarily the ones with schools, have or were in the process of constructing airstrips.

History and Effects of "Contact"

Because they lack a written tradition, it is difficult to place the Huaorani in a long-term historical perspective. It is important to bear in mind that whatever we know about the early history of the Huaorani must be gleaned from the statements of interested outsiders, whether missionaries, colonists, explorers, or most recently, social scientists. In truth, the most dramatic changes in Huao society, at least within the last 100-plus years, have all in some way been precipitated by the activities of "outsiders." The images of the Huaorani as they have been presented to the "outside" are also important because the perceptions of the Huaorani people that have developed over time, particularly during the twentieth century, in the regional, national, and international contexts have had and continue to have a direct impact on the attempts by the Huaorani to organize politically in general and on their organization (ONHAE) on a continuing basis. I will discuss three epochs of "contact" with the Huaorani in more detail: the rubber boom of the late nineteenth and early twentieth centuries; the missionization undertaken in the late 1950s through today by North American based evangelical Christian sects; and the ongoing penetration of the oil industry in Huaorani territory.

The Rubber Boom

The general circumstances of the rubber boom as it affected Ecuador were described above. This period in which the forces of extractive capitalism first penetrated the interior of the Amazon Basin reached and affected the Huaorani in a number of ways. First, the development of more regularized systems of transportation on the rivers, particularly the Napo, meant a fairly constant influx of visitors to the area. Second, the establishment of settlements along these rivers, most notably in and around the modern town of Puerto Francisco de Orellana (known locally as "Coca"), brought the Huaorani into some sort of "contact" with "outsiders" from this period. This meant that certain types of manufactured goods were present among the Huaorani, whether acquired through trade or through raids on the haciendas or work crews (which were forced to spread out throughout the jungle areas). More importantly for the ancestors of the Huaorani, however, was the interaction that took place between themselves and the new invaders of their territory.

Unlike previous incursions, such as those by the early missionaries and explorers, these new entrepreneurs were in the region
(they thought) to stay, and the economic basis for their presence
(the collection and preliminary refining of rubber) necessarily
involved the whole of the surrounding jungle. Additionally, the
collection of rubber is an extremely labor-intensive undertaking
requiring substantial familiarity with the rainforest. The rubber
merchants and *hacendados* needed a great deal of labor and turned
to the indigenous peoples of the region to supply it. The system of
labor that was established, however, was not capitalist wage labor,
but slavery. Indigenous people were captured and sold in slave
markets up and down the Amazon. There are reports that Huaorani people were sold in these markets as well (Cabodevilla 1994:
138; CONAIE 1989: 73). In the Ecuadorian Amazon the bulk of
the indigenous labor force was made up of Quichua and Shuar.

The Huaorani, meanwhile, developed their reputation for
ferocity toward non-Huaorani. Blanca Muratorio (1991: 133-46)
has compiled ethnographic evidence through the oral histories of
former Quichua-speaking rubber tappers of the fear of Huaorani
raiding parties. Additional testimonies (Dall'Alba 1992: 14-17) document Huaorani attacks on rubber haciendas in 1910 and 1950;
in these attacks the raiders made off with manufactured goods
and, interestingly, made a special point of destroying the firearms
of the *hacendados*.

Even the accounts written by evangelical missionaries anxious
to paint the pre-contact Huaorani as savages refer to the slavery
imposed on the Huaorani. They also describe a Señor Sandoval
who already had two captive Huaorani families on his hacienda
and could not understand why their relatives in the forest did not
want to come and "work" for him as well (Elliot 1981: 96-99).

Cabodevilla (1994: 196-98) relates that in 1926 a group of
about seventy Quichua rubber tappers supervised by a young mestizo *hacendado* went in search of new trees in the area between the
Napo and the Cururay rivers (the heart of Huao territory); after
some days they observed the footprints of "savages" and began to
hunt them, presumably to capture them as slaves. Once they began
to actively pursue the "Aucas" they were attacked, and several of
the party were killed. One of the survivors told officials that he had

hidden and seen the Huaorani kill the wounded and captured slowly, while dancing and singing (a highly unlikely tale). Those that survived fled and spread the story of the "savage Aucas," contributing further to the ferocious reputation of the Huaorani in the region.

It is difficult to draw many conclusions about the Huaorani's own perceptions of their experience of the rubber boom period in their territory, but it is clear that at the time it represented the single largest non-Huaorani incursion in the territory in 400 years, and that the Huaorani violently resisted the penetration of their territory. It seems likely to have also exacerbated or reinforced the distrust and fear of *cowode* that was such a salient characteristic of Huao society as recently as twenty years ago. It also marks the beginning of the modern mythology about the Huaorani as violent and "savage," as their raids earned them notoriety throughout the eastern Amazon.

The Interregnum: 1930–1955

By the end of the First World War the British establishment of a plantation system for rubber production in Southeast Asia had brought the price of rubber on the world market crashing down. Although some rubber gathering continued to take place in the Amazon (and continues to this day), the boom was over. Throughout the succeeding years, however, pressures from the "outside" on the Huaorani continued to mount. *Colonos*, or settlers, some originally attracted by the rubber boom, began to establish towns and farms in the area. A war was fought between Ecuador and neighboring Peru, resulting in the loss of about half of the Ecuadorian Amazon to Peru and the subsequent militarization of the area, particularly the rivers. And in 1937 the Shell Oil Corporation began searching for oil in the Ecuadorian Amazon.

The Huaorani reacted to these various assaults on the integrity of their territory with the systematic use of violent resistance. Anyone entering Huao territory–*colono*, hunter, explorer, or missionary – was likely to be killed or otherwise harassed upon discovery. However, the violence perpetrated by the Huaorani on outsiders was not the only violent exchange faced by the Huaorani. In many cases these attacks against interlopers drew retaliation. Outsiders killed many Huaorani in this period and destroyed a number of *nanicabo* settlements. When a community had been the subject of a reprisal raid by outsiders (or if it simply feared that it might be), it would move, abandoning its hunting grounds and plantings; perhaps more importantly, it would attempt to hide in the forest, living in fear for an extended period of time. Additionally, an attack on one's *nanicabo* demanded that action be taken to avenge any deaths. This led to further and more aggressive attacks, and in turn more reprisal raids by *cowode* (Rival 1992: 51-62; Robarchek and Robarchek 1998: 24-27; Yost 1981A: 677-679). In this atmosphere it is not surprising that the violence and fear that had come to characterize Huaorani life in this period spilled over into a surge of violence within and between Huao groups.

This rise in violence helps to explain why the Huaorani eventually accepted the missionary presence in their midst. The missionaries' writings and teachings emphasize the maintenance of the peace. As described earlier in this chapter, James Yost (1981a: 680-681 and 695) has described Huaorani church services as a renewal of the peace between members of the community. It has also helped to provide the necessary "moral" justification for the continuing missionary presence among the Huaorani—as evidenced most clearly in the work of Yost (Yost 1981) who indicates that the Protestant missionaries saved the Huaorani from a self-imposed extinction by ending the cycle of revenge killing. At a time of increasing desperation and fear, the missionaries, if nothing else, preached an end to the violence that had wracked Huao society. The Huaorani had yet to learn that the violence of the *cowode* was of a subtler and ultimately more destructive nature.

The Missionaries

Because missionization has proven to be of such critical importance in the changes that have shaken Huaorani society in the last fifty years, and because the missionaries are so inextricably linked with others who are entering the area, particularly the oil companies, it is important to lay out some basic information about these missionaries before we go any further. Additionally, because for so many people missionary activity provokes a powerful emotional response (pro or con), I will discuss my own views of the missionaries who work with the Huaorani, as well as the missionary enterprise in more general terms.

Missionaries have been a part of the upper Amazon more or less continuously since the arrival of the Spanish in the 1530s. The different generations of missionaries represented an enormous variety of beliefs, methods, and social ideologies. As discussed above, Jesuits, Capuchins, and other Roman Catholic missionary orders were the first to enter the region, but the various governments of Ecuador have permitted Protestant evangelical missionaries to operate in the *oriente* as far back as the period immediately following the change in government of 1912. However, it is not these early missionaries with whom I will be concerned, but rather the relatively recently arriving North American Protestant evangelicals, particularly the Summer Institute of Linguistics and its front organizations (JAARS, Wycliffe Bible Translators, etc.).

The North American evangelical missionaries of the second half of the twentieth century have undoubtedly had a greater impact on Huaorani society than any other outside force. There are many reasons for this powerful impact. Unlike previous outsiders who had come, these missionaries very specifically targeted the Huaorani; they arrived at the moment of the Huaorani people's greatest weakness and fear, and they have stayed in the forest with the Huaorani for longer (now almost forty years) than any other outside group. Moreover, as I will discuss in greater detail below, the missionaries have very effectively made themselves "indispensable" to the Huaorani; using tactics reminiscent of the *reducciones* of the past they have so altered the material conditions of life in the forest that the Huaorani must now depend upon them for their very survival.

Foremost among the groups that have left their mark on the Huaorani (and throughout the upper Amazon) is the Summer Institute of Linguistics (SIL). This organization, founded by William Cameron Townsend in the 1930s, purports to be a scientific organization dedicated to the study of world languages. Also called Wycliffe Bible Translators, the SIL formed (after World War II) the Jungle Aviation and Radio Service (JAARS). When appropriate, the SIL has presented itself as a scientific organization studying the languages of indigenous peoples. In truth, the goals of the SIL are the same as those of other fundamentalist and evangelical mission-aries–conversion to Christianity and the establishment of a funda-mentalist Christian church leadership ("church planting" in the rhetoric of the missionaries). Their "linguistic" work consists almost exclusively of studying indigenous languages for the purpose of creating bible translations. They work to win converts, who they hope will become church leaders and carry forward the evangelical mission. But the Christianity which the SIL brings to indigenous communities goes far beyond mere theological indoctrination. The SIL brings the values of capitalism (including individual wage labor and competitiveness) accompanied by fervent anticommu-nism and a pro-American stance that is communicated as being a necessary component of the process of becoming "Christian." Democracy and capitalism (identified as "free markets" or eco-nomic "freedom") are routinely conflated. As will be discussed below, this anticommunism has taken the form of active discour-agment of any support for liberation and reform movements, even as it strives to garner support for repressive, totalitarian, right-wing regimes in the Americas, Asia, and Africa.

Most of the Protestant evangelical organizations operating in Ecuador, including the SIL, share a theology that is fundamentalist, millenarian, and dispensationalist (Hallum 1996: 48-61). The brand of Protestantism that gave rise to this missionary enterprise was a product of the Protestant movement in the United States. Following the rapid incorporation of small-holding farmers, petty bourgeois merchants, and others into the market-driven economy of the late nineteenth and early twentieth centuries, fundamentalism offered simple and absolute answers to the bewildering circumstances of these elements of American society. Dispensationalism has its roots in the writings of John Nelson Darby, the founder of the Plymouth Brethren (the denomination to which Nate Saint belonged). Dis-pensationalism divides all of time into a series of stages or "dispen-sations." According to this paradigm, God made a series of covenants with the Jews that were intended to produce the kingdom of heaven on earth when the messiah came. When the Jews rejected the messiah, God turned his back on them and built a new covenanted people out of the gentiles. These people are "the Church." God will not deal again with the Jews until his church is complete, at which point all of the members of the church will be "raptured" into heaven. Then, according to the dispensationalists, will come the "end times" described in the bible–the antichrist, the chaining of the devil in hell, and the battle of Armageddon. This, they assert, will be followed by the establishment of the millennial kingdom on earth (Weber, in Reid 1990: 358). Thus the work of the missionaries is designed to help complete the building of "the church" in order to bring about the rapture and end times.

A number of works, of varying degrees of scholarly merit, have examined the work of the SIL. Many (see for example Bamat 1986; Cano et al 1979; Colby and Dennett 1995; Hvalkof and Aaby 1981; Palomino 1980; Pérez and Robinson 1983; Stoll 1982) have seen the SIL as a pawn or tool of U.S. imperialism, and a number of them (including Cano et al 1979; Colby and Dennett 1995; Palomino 1980; and Perez and Robinson 1983) have gone so far as to state that the SIL is an active agent of United States government policy. These works are frequently flawed by a leap from circumstantial evidence showing that the SIL's work has acted to shore up U.S. foreign policy initiatives, to the conclusion that the leaders of the SIL are actually CIA (or, alternatively, Rockefeller family) agents acting under direct orders. Eduardo Galeano (1997: 224-29) sees the American Protestant missionaries as neocolonial agents effectively subduing the Amazon for the more effective exploitation of its raw materials. A few works that make reference to the SIL, particularly those by Christian or relatively more conservative anthropologists (see for example Robarchek and Robarchek 1998 and Yost 1981a) see the SIL as a benign influence. When major works have tried to take on the SIL, its defenders have been quick to find fault with the work. Gerard Colby's meticulously researched account is a case in point – the case that he makes against the SIL is very strong, but he goes one (admittedly logical) step beyond the evidence he has found, and in so doing opens himself up to criticism. I spent a great deal of time speaking with both current and former SIL/JAARS/Wycliffe missionaries and reviewing publications concerning the SIL, and to me it seems largely irrelevant whether the SIL is or is not an active agent of the CIA or any other branch of the U.S. government or ruling class. What is plain is that its actions, whether dictated by some insidious agent of imperialism or self-selected, have served to advance the penetration of global capitalism and U.S. imperialism. The SIL, as a branch of the North American religious right, and the U.S. government share goals and ideology–their beliefs and actions are coterminous rather than necessarily coordinated. From Vietnam, where the SIL actively encouraged the U.S. to step up the campaign against the communist North (Colby and Dennett 1995: 560-75; Stoll 1982: 86-87), to the Philippines, where the SIL supported (hand in hand with the notorious Colonel Edward Lansdale) Magsaysay, to the oilfields of the Amazon, where "hostile" indigenous groups hindered the advance of extractive capitalism, the SIL has always acted to further the interests of the United States' ruling class. This may well be indicative of some sort of relationship between the SIL and the U.S. government, but I doubt that this would extend as far as being actual agents. Research conducted by Stoll (1982) and Colby and Dennett (1995), among others, has failed to find any significant direct evidence that the SIL has acted *directly* as an agent. The most impressive thing about the SIL members that I have met (in the U.S. as well as South America) is their absolute sincerity and passion. What they represent, and what they believe in so fervently, is what seems to have brought their practice of missionary work into such harmony with U.S. interests. I will describe a few of the SIL's activities in this regard, which are illustrative of the sort of coincidence of goals and an opportunistic willingness to accept abuses by the missionary's patrons.

The SIL has not only been anticommunist, but has also systematically opposed peoples' and workers' struggles for better conditions. The SIL in Guatemala in the 1940s and 50s actively urged indigenous Maya to shift from centuries-old traditional cooperative relations of production to wage labor within the framework of capitalist agriculture. They also actively discouraged confrontation or rebellion against exploitative working conditions–the *campesinos* should instead "pray that the bosses would open their hearts to Jesus" (Stoll 1982: 52). In Vietnam the SIL actively supported the U.S. war effort and served, with permission of the U.S. Army, as a propaganda arm helping to "pacify" remote communities where it was feared that the NLF had established a base of support. The SIL also supported the right-wing dictatorship in Cambodia (Stoll 1982: 90-92).

In Africa, at the time of the CIA-orchestrated murder of democratically elected Congolese President Patrice Lumumba, JAARS' chief pilot, Lawrence Montgomery, flew missions for the CIA while still on the rolls of JAARS (Colby: 1996: 340). In South America in particular, the SIL was the advance guard of both capitalist penetration and counterrevolution. As the SIL entered Peru (their first location in Amazonia), they deliberately sought out indigenous people who could be suborned through trade goods and made to accept both Christianity and oil exploration (Stoll 1982: 99-101). They were supported by the neoliberal Peruvian government of Fernando Belaúnde, whose goal was the pacification of the Amazonian indigenous populations, particularly the Matses, in order to make possible the development of the region's oil resources (Colby 1996: 482). The SIL and particularly JAARS helped to assure their continued permission to stay in Peru by ferrying prisoners to a remote penal colony and doing other favors for the government (Stoll 1982: 107). The SIL established schools throughout the Peruvian Amazon with the active support of the Peruvian government. Much of the training in these schools was ideological and religious. As Barbara Bradby (1980: 124) states:

> A large part of the material taught is religious. Protestant hymns are taught with the aid of cassette recorders—the same cassettes that record the last sounds of the indigenous music, doomed to a swift death as the strains of "Onward Christian Soldiers" march in and take over in a symbolic transformation of the whole process.

In Ecuador, and particularly among the Huaorani, the SIL has taken its anticommunist message to include opposition to the struggles of indigenous peoples to organize themselves for political action. The missionaries have denounced OPIP, CONFENIAE, and ONHAE itself as "communist organizations". According to Leonardo Viteri, a Quichua activist and the director of the OPIP affiliated Instituto Amazanga:

> They [the evangelical missionaries] follow a plan of work that is very sophisticated, well-planned, and very right-wing – they speak always

of "communists" and they call the peoples' organizations communist. I see the strong influence that this has on the Huaorani, that they don't feel free, they've been made to accept in a certain manner this way of thinking and they have to liberate themselves from this influence in order to develop a plan of action, a plan of development, that is truly their own.

The SIL has been active in the missionization of many of the indigenous groups of the Ecuadorian Amazon. The Shuar (Jívaro), who formed the first major indigenous organization in the 1960s, have faced continual missionary opposition to the "communist" Federación Shuar. The North American evangelicals have gone so far as to sponsor the creation of a rival conservative Shuar organization in those parts of the Shuar territory that remain firmly under the control of the missionaries (Siracusa 1996: 218-22).

A key component of the success of the SIL is its dissimulation and obfuscation of its true mission. The SIL absolutely sees its goal as the establishment of churches, not just translation of the scripture (Stoll 1982: 113-14). The very processes necessary to the establishment of these churches—first, the translation of the bible; second, the establishment of schools; and third, the establishment of churches with an evangelical mission – are inherently ethnocidal in nature (for discussion see Moore 1981). Through the process of conversion to Christianity itself, the missionaries are destroying a holistic world view and spiritual system that has proved itself to be capable of sustaining the society. Christianity is thus a terribly destructive force in the lives of these "converts." In a Latin American context, the emphasis among U.S.-based Protestant missionaries is on individualism and individual initiative—a destructive view in a society that traditionally stresses "cooperation and reciprocity" (Goffin 1994: 142). Additionally, the missionaries of the SIL systematically advance both monogamy (at least understandable in terms of Christian teachings) and, more importantly in my view, the establishment of the nuclear family as the basis for social production and reproduction (Hvalkof and Aaby, 1981: 176-80). The latter concept is the far more insidious and destructive of the two because it serves to unhinge a society whose material survival is based on sharing and cooperation.[3]

Beyond just the one organization, the missionary enterprise is itself an important issue. The effects of missionary work are very much in the eye of the beholder. The missionaries see their role as the spreading of the word of God, and through their conversions the saving of souls. They see the "unreached tribes" as backward, and the arrival of the Gospel as progress (Swanson 1995: 174). The very nature of their work emphasizes and distorts the strangeness and "otherness" of the people they are supposedly working to help; Swanson (1995: 140) calls it a "fugue of cultural alienation."

In many respects, missionaries represent the antithesis of participant observation; they have no interest in coming to understand the communities of "others" from the inside, except where some knowledge of a society is necessary in order to distort its beliefs. Instead, the primary goal of the missionary enterprise is to convert and fundamentally alter the beliefs and practices of the "other." Missionaries enter a community as foreigners who are materially and spiritually independent of the life of the community, receiving their support from remote and often inexplicable sources, and actively eschewing the beliefs and spiritual comforts of their host communities (until their hosts adopt the Christian faith). Swanson (1995: 19) asserts that this serves to marginalize the missionaries. Certainly they live within a peculiar subculture of missionaries and converted "natives" and ordinarily plan to return to their home country after their "tour of duty."

Missionaries justify their presence through a belief that in presenting the word of Jesus Christ to people who have never heard of him, they will be offering that person the free choice of salvation. Such fundamentalist Christianity, of course, is incapable of seeing itself and its "God" as culturally contingent or socially produced. The combination of religious chauvinism, western bias, naïveté, and contempt toward the societies they enter creates a deadly and ethnocidal mix. These views toward the native subjects of missionization can be seen when Elizabeth Elliot, wife of one of the missionaries killed by the Huaorani, writes:

> In the United States there is usually respect for the word of God–that is, outward respect, even where there is no thought of obedience to it. In the Ecuadorian jungle the indian has not reached that "level of culture"–he has neither respect, manifested by apparent attention when it is being read, nor reverence, manifested in obedience to it. (Elliot 1970: 223)

Or when Jim Elliot, revered as a saintly martyr in evangelical circles, says:

> It is a never ending source of amazement to me how the lofty teach-ings of our Lord–having been fitted to primitive situations –are fre-quently more readily understood by a jungle Indian than by a cultured person who is a product of twentieth-century civilization. (Elliot 1970: 233)

In discussions with the missionaries stationed in Shell-Mera I found a powerful belief in the necessity, the duty, of bringing the Huaorani "out of darkness." Several missionaries very directly and specifically told me that they were sad about Huaorani who had rejected conversion to Christianity because they were destined for hell. Non-missionaries see a much broader view of the impact of missionaries. Elmer Miller (1970) has demonstrated that despite the supernatural nature of the missionary enterprise (conversion to a belief in an alien supernatural system), the Christian missionary is in fact an "agent of secularization" bringing western science, med-icine, and technology, and in most cases displacing (or attempting to displace) holistic supernatural belief systems. The missionaries, and specifically the SIL in Ecuador, have turned traditional society on its head, giving selected converts control over access to medical care, flights, and food, thus creating "culture brokers" and carving out entirely new roles within the social fabric of the community (Pollock 1993: 171-73; Yost 1981a: 693-94). The evangelical mis-sionaries also bring with them a right-wing international and national political agenda, an embrace of capitalist labor relations (linked to wage labor and individualism), and an economic system that is made to seem to be somehow a part of Christianity itself. As stated by John Gledhill (1994: 85): "The missionary project went deeper than simply converting the 'natives' to Christianity. ... [and] was oriented towards inculcating a set of values and disciplines specifically associated with industrial capitalism."

In the end, the missionary enterprise is about ethnocide–the destruction of a people and a way of life. Conversion to an alien religion that in turn is conflated with a different mode of social pro-duction and reproduction and linked to a totalizing world system is pure destruction, the eradication of a people. This is true even

when, as in the case of the SIL, certain discrete components of
the indigenous culture (in this case the language) are preserved.
Jonathan Hill (1999) states that Kuripaka culture was destroyed by
the missions, even as the missions were instrumental in the preservation of Kuripaka language. In the case of the Huaorani there is
also an important distinction to be made between the work of the
foreign (primarily North American) Protestant evangelical missionaries and the work of the Roman Catholic missions in the
region. Influenced by liberal theological trends within the Church,
including the influence of Liberation Theology, much of the work
being undertaken by the Catholic missionaries, particularly the
Capuchin mission in Coca, has been positively beneficial to the
Huaorani. In contradiction to much of the past behavior of the
church, the Catholic missionaries serving the Huaorani seem
utterly uninterested in "conversion" of the Huaorani—on the contrary, the focus of Catholic missionary work has been on preserving and defending the Huaorani culture, people, and territory.

Gray (1997: 76-77) suggests that the missionaries represent an
indispensable aid to the process of penetration and colonization of
the Amazon. When indigenous groups occupying potentially valuable land are identified by a first wave of traders and explorers,
missionaries enter the territory. The missionaries "gradually make
contact with the indigenous peoples of the rainforest and consti-
tutes the buffer between them and the state as a whole." This, in
turn, facilitates the colonization of the region and its true incorporation into the nation-state.

Additionally, although this cannot be said of all missionaries
and in fact has been something many missionary groups have
actively tried to discourage, many missionaries, desperate for new
converts, encourage total dependency on the mission station or the
individual missionary to make it materially impossible for indigenous people to reject their teachings. Such was certainly the case
with Rachel Saint and her followers in the establishment of missionary communities among the Huaorani.

In the case of the Huaorani, the story of evangelical missionization begins with a story of killing. In 1956 a number of different
evangelical Christian missionary organizations were all trying to
discover a way to reach and convert (pacify) the Huaorani. One

group, working as part of the Summer Institute of Linguistics, was led by Rachel Saint. Rachel Saint had one Huaorani refugee, Dayuma, working with her to teach her the language. Her brother, Nate Saint, a pilot with the Missionary Aviation Fellowship (not JAARS, which is an SIL front organization) and a Plymouth Brethren[4] missionary, was in competition with Rachel, trying to reach the "Auca" before her. Nate Saint organized what he called "Operation Auca," flying over the jungle to locate Huaorani settlements and dropping gifts to the villages in a bucket on a rope. With little knowledge of Huao Terero and little advance planning, he and four other missionaries flew in to land on the river near a Huao settlement that they had identified from the air and had dropped gifts to. All of the activities associated with "Operation Auca" were kept secret from anyone not directly involved in the project (Eliot 1970; Hitt 1975: 239), a reflection of the bitter competition among evangelical groups. After they spent one night there, having had at least one peaceful visit with the Huaorani, things turned violent. According to the missionary accounts, the Huaorani mounted an "unprovoked" attack on the men, who, rather than turn their weapons on the Huaorani, permitted themselves to be "martyred." This version has found its way into so many accounts of the incident that by the time I began doing fieldwork I certainly did not believe that it was in dispute. But when a group of young Huao men, including Gilberto Mincaye and Delfin Andy (a Quichua who is married to the daughter of Dayuma), sat down to write a "history of the Huaorani people," to my surprise they wrote that the missionaries had shot one of the Huaorani warriors. They all claimed to have had this information directly from participants in the killings, and seemed to think that it was common knowledge. Whatever took place, the missionaries were all killed, and several days later their bodies and planes were discovered and retrieved (with the help of the U.S. Army's Southern Command in Panama). The news of their "martyrdom" resulted in an outpouring of donations and volunteers.

The chief beneficiary of all of this was Rachel Saint, Nate's sister and former competitor. Rachel, together with Elisabeth Elliot, the widow of one of the missionaries killed along with Nate Saint was already working with Dayuma to learn the rudiments of Huao

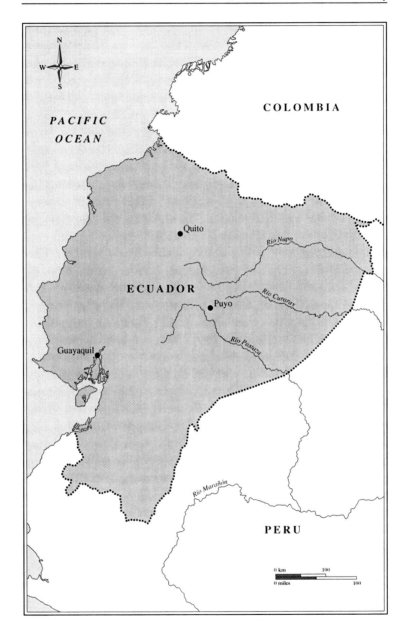

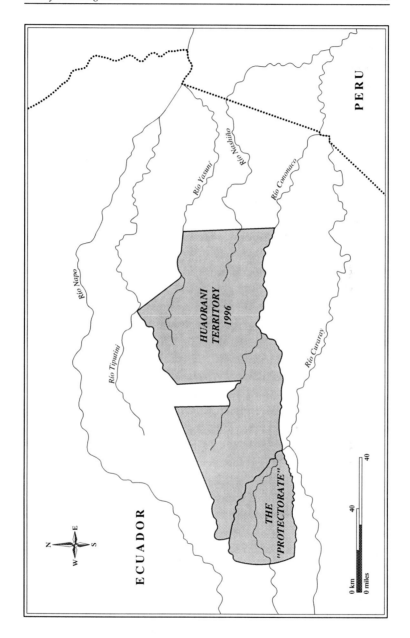

Terero: she began the first pacific contacts with Huaorani communities shortly after the killings.

Largely because of the killings and the attendant publicity, Rachel Saint, now transformed from competitor to posthumous ally and co-worker, became an international hero to the evangelical Protestant movement. She and Dayuma appeared before thousands at Madison Square Garden with the Reverend Billy Graham's "crusade." Rachel was also featured in a Life Magazine story about the killings, and appeared (again with Dayuma) on Ralph Edwards' "This is Your Life" television show. As Rachel Saint and her work became one of the biggest attractions in the world of the evangelicals, her ability to raise money and to act without organizational constraint grew. According to Swanson (1995: 83), many of the North American missionaries working in Ecuador today trace the roots of their "call" to missionary service directly to the "Auca massacre" of 1956.

Rachel stayed with the Huaorani from then on and became very closely identified with them; she always (until 1973) headed up the Huaorani projects of the SIL. The SIL received a government contract creating a "Protectorate" for the Huaorani consisting of an area less than 10 percent of the size of the traditional Huaorani lands. This land was not given directly to the Huaorani; instead, a trust was created under which the SIL would be completely in charge of the land, communities, and people within it.

Using a constant flow of gifts and promises of more, Rachel and the SIL succeeded in drawing the majority of Huaorani to live in the missionary community. In this relocation and concentration project, carried out with the support of the Ecuadorian government and military as well as direct financial support for operations paid from the Texaco-Gulf oil development consortium to the SIL, the SIL and Rachel Saint deliberately moved the Huaorani off of and away from petroleum rich areas (Goffin 1994: 67-73). The community established by Rachel Saint was centered around education, specifically religious education. Cabodevilla (1994: 383-89) has deliberately used the word "*reducción*" (the Spanish equivalent of reservation) to describe the SIL's activities in the Protectorate, thus choosing to equate the SIL's activities with the genocidal policies of the seventeenth- and eighteenth- century Spanish colonizers of the region. Fundamentalist evangelical Christianity was (and is) taught in the schools of the Protectorate (along with a virulent anticommunism), and the rules laid down by Rachel Saint had to be obeyed. These rules included monogamy (which forced Huaorani to abandon second wives and their children), the use of clothing provided by the mission at all times, and labor under the supervision of the missionaries. Construed in the most positive light, these things, controlled and administered by foreigners and operated with the sanction of the state in the background, would be terribly destructive.

Missionization had many other effects as well. First, the missionaries failed to mount an organized campaign of vaccinations, while at the same time concentrating the population in a small area with inadequate sanitation. Predictably, a series of epidemics swept through the population (the most serious being a polio epidemic in 1969), leaving many dead and others permanently disabled. Second, as a result of attempts to curb the regular nomadic movements of family groups, and because of the concentration of the population in one place, the area surrounding the mission suffered from overhunting. As the area's game was depleted, men had to go farther and farther afield to hunt, until finally it became impossible for the men to provide their families with meat without traveling for days. One of the many consequences of this change was a hardening of gender roles as women were required to stay in the community to care for the gardens and the children, while groups of men were absent on hunting trips for ever greater periods of time. The most serious repercussion of the depletion of the game was that once meat was no longer readily available, the Huaorani became absolutely dependent on the missionaries for their very survival. Any act of rebellion or disobedience might cause the expulsion of a family from the missionary-sponsored community. Rachel Saint controlled the Protectorate as her personal fiefdom, refusing to let anyone visit without her permission, and even refusing to help the Ecuadorian military conduct a census of the Huaorani.

However, it is important to bear in mind that the Huaorani certainly wanted the goods that were made available to them through contact with the missionaries. Aluminum cooking utensils have now almost completely eliminated traditional Huaorani ceramics, and machetes, steel axes, outboard motors, and "store-bought" food (rice, tuna, sugar, Yupi) are highly sought after. Shotguns are popular but show no signs of replacing blowguns for a variety of reasons (see Yost 1983). As Kensinger (1999, personal communication) says of the Cashinahua of Peru: "whatever one's opinion of the missionary enterprise, it cannot be denied that the Cashinahua aggressively pursued the trade goods offered by contact". This in turn reflects a sort of cultural ambivalence that is common among Amazonian groups. Gray (1997: 226-67) describes this contradiction among the Arakmbut of Peru: "The Arakmbut are proud of having successfully preserved their language, their knowledge and their traditions. On the other hand, they often feel inferior to other indigenous peoples who can manage the world dominated by the Peruvian national society more smoothly."

Over time Rachel Saint and the SIL received a great deal of criticism for their stewardship of the Protectorate. Finally, in the early 1970s the SIL sent James Yost, an anthropologist but also an evangelical Christian and SIL member, to investigate Rachel Saint's work. Yost had spent more than a decade working with the Huaorani, was fluent in Huao Terero, and had published a number of works on the group (Cf. Kaplan and Yost 1984; Yost 1983, 1981a, 1981b). Despite his presumably mixed allegiances, Yost produced a report that was highly critical of Saint and the conduct of the mission. Under pressure, Rachel Saint rejected the calls to work against Huaorani dependency, and in 1976 the SIL ordered her into retirement. Shortly afterwards, in 1981, the organization was officially expelled from the country (Goffin 1994: 73). This, however, did not deter Rachel Saint, who went back to the United States and hit the lecture circuit. Having obtained funding from an evangelical church in Oklahoma, she returned to Ecuador, and resumed her work with the Huaorani, now without the official imprimatur of the SIL. In truth, the SIL did not leave the country. Their missionaries continued their work, operating in the same manner as before, under a variety of different names and providing extensive material support for Rachel Saint's (now unaffiliated) work. Rachel Saint continued her work until she died, in Toñampade, in November of 1995.

Today the work of the missionaries continues in the Protectorate, funded by a number of evangelical missionary organizations and churches. Rachel Saint's house and grave are simultaneously treated as shrines and largely ignored by the Huaorani members of the community. Although many Huaorani have left the missionary-dominated community of Toñampade, young people who wish to continue their education must still live there for a number of years, as it contains the only high school in Huaorani territory. High school students, who come from communities throughout the territory, live in dormitories near the airstrip and receive their education for free. But this education is limited, and the focus is as much on evangelical religion as it is on skills and knowledge. To date, no Huaorani has attended any college or university, and the high school is almost completely male – at the time of my fieldwork only one Huao woman had graduated from the high school. The schools in the territory remain completely dominated by the missionaries. Despite a national campaign to encourage bilingual schools utilizing indigenous languages for the majority of instruction, the missionaries have been generally hostile to the idea. Additionally, the missionary schools are run according to strict evangelical guidelines. One Huaorani school, for instance, was closed and all further funding cut off after it was discovered that dancing had been permitted in the school building. It should be noted that dancing and chanting are central to Huaorani cultural expression.

In the schools one can see clearly the ambivalent links between the missionaries, the Huaorani, and the oil companies. Many of the buildings that make up the school were built or repaired by the oil companies and have the oil companies' logos painted on them – Petroecuador (the state-run oil enterprise) and Maxus appear in this way. The building supplied by Maxus contains a mural celebrating the "*convenio*" between Maxus and ONHAE, the Huaorani organization founded with the express purpose of fighting against the missionaries. The missionaries have close and cordial links with the oil companies and help them to recruit Huaorani to work on the exploration projects and cut paths through the jungle for seismic testing. As stated by Siracusa (1996: 255): "[T]he Huaorani were well on their way to integration with the global economy, particularly with the help of missionaries who supported their involvement with the transnational oil companies."

One missionary who continues in Huaorani territory is Stephan Saint, the son of Nate Saint, who grew up with the Huaorani but has adopted an attitude of superiority toward them. He has established himself as the leader of a small community of Huaorani, where he, like his aunt before him, makes all of the rules. He is the minister of the church in the community and does not seem to have made any effort to establish indigenous church leadership, as most evangelical missions at least attempt to do. In his community he has stressed the importance of capitalist relations of production and distribution. He has established his own store and "sells" (for town scrip) everything in it–he told me that in that way he can avoid creating dependence on the missionary trade goods that had characterized his aunt's project. He also operates a logging enterprise, a bakery, and other income-generating activities. However, in reality what he is doing is implementing capitalist relations of employment and distribution, and in the process, sanctifying them with a religious/missionary imprimatur. One young man, Mincaye, who has defied Saint by becoming an activist in ONHAE (and was elected *conserje* at the 1996 *Biye*), moved to Nemonpade from Toñampade with his family when he was a boy:

> We moved to Nemonpade because the gringo [Stephen Saint] offered many things and my parents said "we're going there," but when we went there he offered all those things, he said he would fly us for free when we needed it, but later when we wanted a flight to bring some food in he said no. And we said "what are we going to do now" and he told us that he would give us some things but that we had to buy them from him. And my parents are still working for him to pay off the things he gave them. They work for him, and my 11-year-old sister; he didn't give anything.

The Oil Boom

Successive Ecuadorian governments, civilian and military, have used oil in their discourse as the centerpiece of national economic development planning. Oil has been the collateral for loans and international bailouts, has been used to lure international investment, and has become part of the nationalist rhetoric of Ecuador as an "Amazonian Nation" (Bocco 1987: 41-57 and passim; Martz

1987: 352-54 and 370-95). Competing elements of the national bourgeoisie have promoted contradictory oil development policies, with varying degrees of foreign capital participation (Cueva 1982: 97-103).

Oil exploration has a long history in the Ecuadorian Amazon. In 1937 Royal Dutch Shell began a comprehensive program of oil exploration, including some work in Huaorani territory, that resulted in the confirmation that, indeed, the *oriente* held great quantities of underground oil. However, in 1950 Shell decided that the costs of extracting and transporting the oil (over the Andes Mountains) were prohibitive. Subsequently, a contract was awarded to Texaco to build a pipeline over the mountains from Lago Agrio to Esmereldas, a port on the Pacific coast, together with Petroecuador. The pipeline was completed in 1972, and oil began to flow from Texaco's huge refinery. Initially the oil came from the areas surrounding Lago Agrio and Shushufindi, well north of Huaorani territory, but the push for more oil led searchers further south, and the government of Ecuador divided up the *oriente* into a series of numbered exploration blocks and auctioned these blocks off to a number of international oil companies. Part of the reason for the oil companies' initial hesitancy to conduct sustained exploration projects in Huaorani territory was the threat of the Huaorani's famed hostility toward outsiders. In fact, in 1973 the Huaorani killed a Texaco oil drilling and exploration crew and destroyed their helicopter. Later, they also attacked a group of workers from Braspetro, a Brazilian oil company that had purchased exploration rights to one of the blocks in the *oriente*. All of these attacks were widely reported in the Ecuadorian media and many became news around the world, further contributing to the image of the Huaorani as a "savage tribe" that had not yet been brought under the influence of the "civilizing" missionaries (Rival 1994; Siracusa 1996: 46-8).

In the late 1980s the Conoco oil company purchased the rights to the exploration blocks that comprise most of the Huaorani territory. The oil in Block 16 has been estimated to have a value in excess of four billion dollars (Reid 1995: 198). In an attempt to avoid the kind of criticism from environmentalists that Texaco had experienced, they enlisted the Natural Resources Defense Council and its most famous representative, Robert F. Kennedy Jr., to devise a plan for the protection of the region's environment and indigenous people. The company also hired SIL-affiliated anthropologist James Yost to conduct an assessment of the impact that the proposed project would have on the Huaorani, a report that drew bitter criticism from environmentalists, anthropologists, and missionaries alike (Kane: 1995; Kimmerling 1991; Rival: 1992). The NRDC designed a fund for the indigenous people, and a series of environmental safeguards and inspections. However, they did this without the involvement of the Huaorani, and it was partly word of the proposed agreement on their behalf that led the Huaorani to form ONHAE in the first place. When the Huaorani protested the deal that had been negotiated between the NRDC and the oil company, Conoco withdrew from the project and relinquished its contract with the Ecuadorian government for the block (for a full description see Kane 1995; also Kimmerling 1991).

Finally, the Maxus Energy corporation of Houston purchased the rights to Block 16 in the heart of Huaorani territory and began work there; its first wells were completed in 1992. But Maxus was different from other oil companies. First, its corporate leadership was made up of evangelical Christians who immediately went about establishing very close relations with Rachel Saint and the other North American missionaries working in the territory. Second, before the first Maxus oil worker set foot in the territory the company had established the "Departamento de Relaciones Comunitarias" (Department of Community Relations), whose purpose was to handle the company's relations with the Huaorani and others. This department is currently headed by Milton Ortega and Rene Espín; Ortega claims to be an anthropologist. As will be discussed in Chapters 3 and 4, Maxus has largely succeeded in co-opting several successive generations of Huaorani organizational leadership.

Although Ecuador desperately needs oil revenue in order to maintain its debt payments to the U.S. and multilateral lending institutions, the terms of its agreement with Maxus are startlingly bad. Maxus does not begin to pay any royalties on its production until it has fully recovered all of its production and exploration costs. This means that the Ecuadorian government will not see one royalty check until the costs of Maxus' road and pipeline construction, its relocations of American oil workers, every expense, have been recouped (Reid 1995: 201-2).

Oil drilling, like most of the industries representative of extractive capitalism, is tremendously destructive, and Maxus' operations in Ecuador's Amazon are no exception. First, it is necessary to construct a network of roads throughout the area. These roads, even in the best of circumstances, inevitably lead poor people searching for land into the area. Additionally, road construction breaks the forest canopy over extended areas, which serves to isolate populations of arboreal species such as the monkeys upon which the Huaorani depend for their meat protein. According to Delanie Kellon (1996, personal communication), a forestry expert with the Yasuní research station, the Maxus roads have already wreaked havoc with the monkey and sloth populations of the area. (Centro Para Derechos Económicos y Sociales 1994: 34-39; Villamil 1995: 341-42)

The roads constructed by Maxus are (for the moment) regularly patrolled by Maxus security guards, who have so far prevented *colonos* from establishing themselves in Huaorani territory by way of the road. But this watchfulness serves another of the company's purposes: it has kept the company's activities hidden from the prying eyes of the public. Without a company-issued pass, no one may use the road or get anywhere near their oil drilling operations. I myself was "arrested" and questioned by company security guards, who expelled me from the area even though I was traveling with two Huaorani men. And serious questions remain over what will happen along the road when Maxus leaves the region.

Second, the waste products produced by drilling contaminate the environment, particularly the groundwater supplies. Maxus claims that it uses the latest technology to protect the environment around its drilling operations. This includes the "reinjection" of drilling waste into the ground to minimize environmental damage. However, I spoke with a number of oil workers, some of whom had worked for Maxus, and all of whom stated unequivocally that Maxus was leaving the oil waste and toxic "drilling mud" in open pits in the ground.

Third, the workers themselves bring with them the full component of disruptive western social practices – drunkenness, prostitution, and exploitation. Oil workers from Maxus, as well as the other oil companies, have introduced alcohol to the Huaorani. Unlike the staple beverages of some surrounding indigenous groups, the tepe that is the high carbohydrate mainstay of the Huao diet has only a negligible quantity of alcohol, so the stronger spirits brought by the workers have significant potential as a disruptive element. The oil workers have also attempted to lure Huaorani women into prostitution although reports vary over whether this has actually succeeded.

Oil has come to be one of the defining elements of cultural change and development among the Huaorani. The dual penetration of extractive capitalism and foreign evangelical missionaries has led to the erosion of traditional Huaorani cultural practices. More importantly, the Huaorani people have come to live in great uncertainty about their place in the world and the relative value of their own culture and practices.

Relations with Other Indigenous Peoples

At least in their present territory, the Huaorani have as neighbors the Quichua, Shuar, and Zaparoan indigenous communities. But the Huao Terero language contains very few borrowed words, perhaps indicating that the extent of contact and intermarriage with these groups was minimal. Blanca Muratorio (1991: esp. 133-40) has documented that the Quichua and others who worked as rubber tappers at the beginning of the century were terrified of the Huaorani and entered their territory with great trepidation. Although neighbors, they seem to have had little knowledge of the Huaorani, and referred to them as savages ("Auca").

In recent history the relations between the different indigenous peoples of the region have become more cordial, but other groups in the area have become jealous of the size of the Huaorani territory. This has resulted in a desire among neighboring Shuar and Quichua to have Huaorani "godchildren," which is usually understood to grant hunting rights in Huao territory to the godparents. There has also been an increase in intermarriage, particularly between Huaorani women and Quichua men. In a number of instances *colonos* have attempted to establish themselves within the boundaries of Huaorani land and been met with violent expulsion by the Huaorani. In November of 1995, a group of Shuar colonists were reported to have been killed by Huaorani from the village of Quehueire Ono. Although I was not able to conclusively verify that these killings took place, I did speak at different times to a number of Huaorani men who claimed to have participated in the raid, and all agreed that the killings had taken place. I also spoke with some members of the Federación Shuar who had heard of the incident, believed it to be true, and were quite angry about it.

A new source of tension between the Huaorani and other indigenous groups are the relationships between ONHAE and the organizations representing other groups, as well as the provincial, regional, and national organizations of which ONHAE is a member. While I was doing my fieldwork, a dispute over the payment by ONHAE for repair work on an airplane owned by the Organización de los Pueblos Indígenas de Pastaza (OPIP, a Quichua dominated provincial organization) kept the two groups from participating in a number of proposed joint projects. Importantly, the agreements that have been negotiated between ONHAE and the oil companies have been seen by leaders of other indigenous groups as seriously under-cutting their bargaining positions in talks with oil interests. Similarly, ONHAE, as will be discussed in chapters 3 and 4, has been slow to utilize the resources offered by some of the other organizations, particularly the experienced negotiators of the Instituto Amazanga and the political clout that has been developed by CON-FENIAE and CONAIE (respectively the regional and national indigenous federations).

Notes

1. "Auca" is a Quichua word meaning savage or killer. For years the Huaorani were known throughout Ecuador and in missionary and adventurer's writings by this derogatory term.
2. Based on the lack of immunity observed during the twentieth-century epidemics that swept through the Huaorani communities after the arrival of the missionaries.
3. One of the shocking things about Toñampade, the center of missionary activity in the old "Protectorate," is that many of the homes are closed and locked with padlocks and hasps–an unthinkable occurrence in any other Huaorani community.
4. The so-called Plymouth Brethren are a Protestant sect that originated in Ireland at the beginning of the nineteenth century. They are an extremely rigid millennial group whose practices are particularly conservative. For example, women members are not permitted to speak or participate in worship services.

Chapter 2

ONHAE
Structures and Achievements

The organization that is the focus of this work has emerged from a variety of disparate influences. It has thrust the Huaorani into the center of the struggles to preserve tropical rainforests around the world and the struggles to define the future of Ecuadorian and South American political life, as well as the worldwide struggles of indigenous peoples. Yet ONHAE has remained very much a local and a personal organization, dominated by individual personalities, and it has changed policies rapidly under competing pressures from outside forces.

As indigenous people around the globe have attempted to organize to protect their territories and rights, they have been confronted by a multitude of obstacles. Some have been the usual stumbling blocks placed in the path of all subaltern groups whenever they have tried to claim their rights, but others have been unique to the situations of indigenous people. As indigenous people who continue to be part of a system of social production and reproduction different from that of the surrounding national and regional societies (both mestizo and indigenous), the Huaorani continue to depend on their gardens and hunting for most of their sus-

Notes for this section begin on page 101.

tenance. They continue to live in relative isolation, if not from contact with the outside world, then certainly still from the economic and social structures of global capitalism and so-called "third-world" or peripheral (under)development.

When the Huaorani took the step of creating a formal organization to represent (ostensibly) the interests of the Huaorani people, they necessarily entered into a world view based on laws, contracts, courts, and most of all, money and capital. This traditionally leaderless and loosely organized people had to create an entity that could speak with authority for the entire group, negotiate and finalize agreements with outsiders, and operate within the recognized patterns of behavior for such groups. Thus there is an inherent contradiction between the need for a structured, officially recognized group of leaders capable of speaking for the entire group, and the traditionally acephalous, egalitarian structure of Huaorani society. The failures that have been experienced by ONHAE are the result of a combination of factors. But no factor has been more important than the cultural and social gulf that exists between the Huaorani and the national and international contexts in which they are forced to conduct their business. In these contexts the Huaorani's own culture has been skillfully turned against them and used by the oil companies to pervert the efforts of ONHAE.

The creation of a "pan-Huaorani" organization necessarily invokes a "pan-Huaorani" consciousness, and a realization that all of the Huaorani share aspects of a common identity. It has become possible for the Huaorani to define themselves as a people (beyond the extended family or *nanicabo*) only as increased contact with non-Huaorani has created a realization of their commonality in the face of what they are not. Robarchek and Robarchek (1998: 168-70) suggest that the creation of ONHAE represents an important step in the process of "ethnogenesis" (defined in the Introduction). Other institutions implicated in this process include Huaorani intramural soccer teams, the Huaorani educational system, particularly the one high school that serves all Huaorani communities, and the radio network facilitating communication and the spread of news and gossip among most of the various Huaorani communities.

Certainly ONHAE could only have become possible in the context of greater contacts with and understanding of the "outside" world; thus certain elements had to be present in order to create the sort of ethnic consciousness that resulted in ONHAE. Among the necessary elements were: first, greater contact between different Huaorani groups; second, increased nonviolent contacts with an increasing variety of nonHuaorani; and finally, a more or less universal school system operating throughout Huaorani territory. The example of the successful indigenous organizations of Amazonian Ecuador, and of the "ethnic entrepreneurs" at the helm of the indigenous movement, clearly provided an important contextual backdrop. Although ONHAE is only very tenuously articulated with the broader indigenous movement in Ecuador, it is clear that it is the example of that movement that guided its formation.

Regarding the conduct and practice of the organization specifically, this chapter will present a brief organizational history of ONHAE and a description of some of the group's accomplishments in its early years; it will also closely examine the multiple and frequently countervailing articulations of ONHAE's leadership with the non-Huaorani actors with whom they interact. The bulk of the time and work of the leadership of ONHAE takes place in and around the organization's offices in Shell-Puyo, where these leaders are the only Huaorani present for miles. They depend on their non-Huaorani staff for much assistance in negotiating the political and financial intricacies of the organization's daily business activities, and on contacts, formal and informal, with other indigenous leaders for an understanding of politics. This is in addition to highly problematic relationships with the other principal actors: the oil companies, the missionaries, and the environmentalists.

ONHAE's Founding

The impetus for the creation of a Huaorani organization arose during the 1980s. Several factors came together at this time, resulting in the official creation of the organization in 1989-90. The organization itself was formally constituted at a Biye[1] in March of 1990 and at this time took its name: the *Organización de las Nacionalidades Huaorani de la Amazonia Ecuatoriana* or ONHAE[2].

The first factor leading to the creation of ONHAE was the existence of a core group of young males who had been schooled in the mission schools of Tihueno, Toñampade, and Quihuaro. These young men were more aware than their elders of the workings of the white and mestizo world. They had all visited the towns of the Ecuadorian *oriente,* and some had visited Quito. They all spoke adequate (and in some cases excellent) Spanish and could read and write. Some of them had taken sporadic wage labor, working for the oil exploration companies, road builders, and others. In interviews with this original group of founders, each described a feeling that someone who understood both worlds needed to work as the go-between for the Huaorani people. As stated by Enquere, one of the founders:

> The Huaorani, the old warriors, they were just thinking about hunting and fishing for themselves. And we [young men] had decided to say how we wanted to negotiate, and we had to learn how to negotiate with the [oil] company so that it wouldn't be so very difficult. ... and we had to learn how to confront the authorities and speak properly to them and still have their respect.

The second factor was the gradual lessening of the power of the missionaries over the Huaorani. Throughout the 1960s all contact between the Huaorani and non-Huaorani was at least mediated, and more often controlled, by the missionaries of the Summer Institute of Linguistics (SIL), and particularly Rachel Saint. The government of Ecuador ceded administrative control over the Huaorani "Protectorate" directly to the missionaries, who controlled all access to the communities by airplane, controlled what was taught at the schools, and controlled individual behavior through expulsions and threats of expulsion from the communities under their control. The missionaries frequently denounced the organizations (such as the Shuar and Quichua organizations) of indigenous people as "communist" and forbade Huaorani cooperation with those groups. However, beginning in the 1970s the control of the SIL began to slip. This first occurred as a result of the SIL's James Yost's 1973 report on Rachel Saint's activities and her expulsion from the SIL (see previous chapter). The subsequent expulsion from Ecuador of the SIL itself as a formal entity resulted in the further fragmentation of missionary activities in and out of the Protectorate. Finally, the increasing "cultural literacy" of the younger generation of Huaorani, who were beginning to see the rejection of the missionaries as a viable alternative, helped to generate the formation of Quehueire Ono and a renewed pride in Huaorani culture and identity throughout Huaorani territory.

The third factor facilitating the formation of ONHAE was the increasing influence of non-Huaorani, non-evangelical outsiders concerned for the future of the Huaorani people. This included the arrival of Laura Rival, a French anthropologist who was the first to carry out long-term research among the Huaorani without missionary affiliation. Also, representatives of CONFENIAE, CONAIE, and OPIP[3] began to encourage the Huaorani to affiliate formally with them. In July of 1987 CONFENIAE actually held a large meeting and workshop in Toñampade to discuss the possibilities and procedures for getting the Huaorani to organize, but without any immediate results.

The example provided by other indigenous NGOs cannot be overstated. Ecuador is notable for the relative strength of its indigenous organizations. Beginning in 1964 with the founding of the Federación Shuar, organizations inspired by the socialist struggles in Latin America and by civil rights organizations around the world were founded by most of the ethnic groups in Ecuador. These groups in turn formed regional and national federations. They built an organizational base on their demands for land titling and self-determination. They were effective enough that in the 1980s conservative Ecuadorian President Febres Cordero tried to form a parallel organization (*Jatun Ayllu* or "Big Family") in order to sap some of their power (Selverston 1995: 131-141). Andrew Gray (1997: 9-13) also sees the North American and Australian (aboriginal) civil rights movements as providing inspiration to the creation of the indigenous movement. MacDonald (1995a) posits the necessity of external, analogous examples for the initial impetus to organize—certainly in Ecuador the presence of other ethnic-based federations provided the example as well as direct guidance and assistance for the formation of ONHAE.

The last factor leading to the creation of ONHAE was the sense of crisis that resulted from increasingly frequent encroachments on traditional Huaorani lands. Oil companies (notably Texaco, Petroecuador, Unocal, and Petro-Canada) were conducting large-scale oil exploration projects, including seismic tests, and this was having a direct impact on the Huaorani. As the oil companies built roads (particularly the "Via Auca" at the eastern end of the Huaorani's traditional territory), colonists entered in search of land and began clearing tracts in the forest. Tourists also began to enter Huaorani territory at this time (the 1970s and 1980s).

In 1986 A group of individuals, all very young, male, educated in the missionary schools and literate in Spanish, began to talk about forming an organization. Moi, Nanto, Enquere, and Amo were the first generation of leaders. The four were all distant cousins, and although they had not grown up closely the fact of relatedness facilitated those initial contacts and discussions.

The relative youth of these founders of ONHAE is important, and follows the same pattern seen among the Kayapo of the Brazilian Amazon. Turner (1995) states that a young generation of leaders emerged among the Kayapo who were more effectively intercultural than their predecessors. Turner states that this group "used their command of Portuguese and their familiarity with Brazilian ways as a base of political influence" (1995: 15).

Moi is unique among the original leadership of the group, for a number of reasons. First, he actively rejects the teachings of the *evangelicos* and has self-consciously tried to revive traditional Huaorani practices, including shamanic and cosmological belief systems. It is not surprising that he and his family (Moi remains unmarried and lives in the *nanicabo* of his father) live in Quehueire Ono, where he is the only Huao who has made an effort to apprentice himself to Mengotohue, the last true Huaorani "jaguar shaman" living today. It was Moi who revived the practice of wearing hair long in the traditional manner (the missionaries encouraged short hair), and who has fought continuously against not only the oil companies but the missionaries as well. It is important to note, however, that while Moi is frequently quoted as an authority by those studying the Huaorani (Kane 1993, 1995; Siracusa 1996; *Trinkets and Beads* 1996), his support among the Huaorani people is quite limited. This was demonstrated at the 1996 Huaorani assembly or *Biye* (see Chapter 3).

Enquere is in many ways the most "westernized" of the original Huaorani leadership. He is completely fluent and comfortable in Spanish and is accustomed to thinking in terms of calendar dates, years, etc. He has been working for years to try to become a licensed pilot. Yet Enquere, like Moi, has also consistently worked to try to revive traditional Huao culture. Enquere states:

> Before it was an obligation to believe like the evangelicals. But now it is prohibited to be forced to believe any particular way. That's an internal rule that I made when I was President, I made it like that. They [the missionaries] said to leave the culture because somebody says "behave yourself" because their book says, the bible says that you can't go without clothes, put on your clothes even if they are sweaty because you have to. And when I am in my house why do I have to put on clothes. ... It's sad. The Huaorani had changed completely. Why did they say that God doesn't want you to participate in your own culture? That is why I started to study the culture and I worked every night with a cassette recorder and now we have recovered some of our culture.

Nanto, who still lives in the missionary center of Toñampade, is not as comfortable as the others in the world of the *cowode*, and is frequently hostile when asked questions. Among Huaorani, however, he is a practical joker and a hard worker.

I was not able to know Amo, the fourth of the founding members of ONHAE because of his untimely death. It has been suggested by some that his death—which came about while he was riding on the roof of a bus out of Coca—was a murder. There were some suspicious circumstances surrounding his death (see Kane 1995: 152-4), but there is little proof of foul play.

After a period of years in which sporadic discussions went on, a series of formal meetings were held, and then *Biyes* (large group meetings including representatives from different communities) took place in both Quehueire Ono and Toñampade. By now, anthropologist Laura Rival was living and conducting fieldwork in Quehueire Ono and took an active part in the creation of the organization. She told me, and other sources confirmed, that she was instrumental in getting the Huaorani in touch with OPIP and CONFENIAE representatives who provided an intensive leadership training course for the new leaders when they were finally selected in March of 1990. The first officers of the organization were Nanto (elected president over a candidate supported by Rachel Saint); Moi, chosen to be the vice president; Amo, elected secretary; and Enquere, the organization's first treasurer. According to Enquere and others, there was in practice very little specialization of the work among the leadership of the organization. Initially the organization had no telephone, no office, and no formal legal recognition of its role. The newly elected leaders were taken to Puyo and Quito to attend leadership training classes sponsored by CONFENIAE and CONAIE. A close relationship was initially established between the new organization and the leadership of OPIP and CONFENIAE, and Laura Rival served as a constant resource during this first year of organization.

From the very beginning of the organization's existence, pressure was brought to bear on the new leaders of ONHAE. This seems to have shaped the group's institutional relationship with the oil companies right from the beginning. As observed by OPIP's Leonardo Viteri in 1996:

> I believe that the Huaorani people, in the first place, have only just begun to organize themselves. Just in the nineties and precisely [because of] the initiative of CONFENIAE. The leaders since then have begun organizing. Then, when they were just beginning, just one or two years after they started the organization, they had the presence of Maxus, so that they never were able to consolidate the organization before that happened. For us it is still an organization that is just beginning. Much is still lacking for the Huaorani people to be able to consolidate their organizing process with enough clarity.

During Nanto's administration in ONHAE's first years as a formally constituted organization, The Huaorani organized a march to Quito (1992), where they camped on the streets outside of the offices of Maxus and Petroecuador, the state oil company. This encampment, although it lasted for only a week, drew extensive national and international publicity to the case of the Huaorani and earned them a meeting with the then President of the Republic, Sixto Duran Bellen. After these dramatic attempts to say no to the oil companies, Nanto went ahead and signed the first pact between the Huaorani organization and Maxus. The agreement, dated 9 September 1992, gave Maxus the right to build roads in

Huaorani territory in exchange for the construction of a school building and the provision of certain medicines. According to everyone except Nanto, this agreement was arrived at in secret and in direct contradiction of the previous *asemblea's* instructions, that the leadership make no agreements with the company. Evidence collected by journalist Joe Kane (1995: 204-18) and corroborated in my interviews with Enquere and Moi indicates that Nanto accepted a cash bribe offered through a Maxus employee. Nanto denied to me the existence of any such agreement with Maxus in the first place.

In February of 1993 new elections were held at a *Biye* that took place, once again, at Toñampade. Two published accounts of this event exist–one by Joe Kane, which appeared in 1995 and was thus available to me during my fieldwork and interviews, and a second published by Robarchek and Robarchek in 1998 (64-69), which was not. My original information on this important event comes from interviews conducted with leaders and delegates who attended and whom I asked about the accuracy of Kane's account. In general, the interviewed subjects were in agreement with Kane on the events of the *Biye*, Enquere's election platform, and the participation and active support of Maxus, which some did not see as compromising at all. There was some question regarding how many of the delegates participated in a walkout over the issue of oil exploitation.

At this *Biye*, Enquere was elected president on the promise that he would renounce the agreement that Nanto had made with Maxus and renegotiate a new and better one. Ironically, the *Biye* itself was a Maxus-sponsored event. The company paid for the flights to Toñampade as well as the food and drink for the delegates. A number of Maxus representatives, most notably Milton Ortega of the Department of Community Relations, attended and took active roles in the proceedings. A number of delegates (opinions vary about the percentage) concerned about the influence of Maxus and led by Moi, walked out of the *Biye* completely. Despite Enquere's election on a platform of opposition to the further activities of Maxus in Huaorani territory, a resolution permitting Maxus' operations in Huaorani territory was approved overwhelmingly (Robarchek and Robarchek 1998: 66-67). Six months later, on 13 August, 1993, Enquere signed a new "*convenio*"[4] with the company.

The new *convenio*, which was in effect while I conducted my fieldwork, is a vague and dissembling document. It calls upon the company to "listen" with a "positive attitude" to the Huaorani and to participate in "community development." Where specific areas are mentioned, they represent small and inexpensive contributions to be made by the company. According to the document, the company will train community health care workers and teachers, provide vaccinations and emergency treatment, transport teachers to the communities, construct school buildings, and limit the access of colonists to the Maxus road. The budget accompanying the document projects expenditures by the company in fulfillment of the *convenio* in excess of $260,000 in the first year and more than $300,000 in the second year (figures are in U.S. dollars). In practice the company has not spent more than a few thousand dollars in fulfillment of its promises, but has nonetheless begun the extraction of oil valued at many millions of dollars. A few school buildings have been constructed, but these are rather shoddy wooden structures on raised platforms rather than cement buildings with a solid foundation; such buildings have only a very limited life expectancy in the humid jungle environment. During my time in Puyo-Shell, I personally witnessed six cases in which Huaorani were turned away from the (missionary-operated) Hospital Vozandes due to their inability to pay. In a number of cases I paid for Huaorani to receive care, and I came to realize that the costs at the missionary hospital are minimal (for example, $6-12 for a complete set of diagnostic tests). Nancy, Dayuma's daughter and the vice president for health of ONHAE, frequently complained that the company had not trained health workers as promised and had not provided the medicines, vaccinations, and other health care called for in the agreement.

When asked about the agreement with Maxus, Enquere said:

> I didn't want to negotiate. I always do what the people tell me. The people have to decide. Afterward people said that I made the agreement but I said "No, I can only do what you tell me to do." ... Then they [the company] said to me that it was too expensive, what we wanted, and I told them, "If it's too expensive then leave us in peace." ... Then I invited the head of Maxus, Hutton, to come in to a meet-

ing, and then he [Hutton] said that he was in agreement on all the things, and we signed that and [an agreement] to pay for the hospital.

I also asked Enquere what he thought of the *convenio* now. He replied: "I believe that the contract was an error. It is not good. It was a mistake."

Armando Boya, president of ONHAE during my fieldwork, sees a more sinister explanation of the signing of the agreements by Nanto and Enquere. About Nanto he says that:

> In Nanto's time he made a contract, I have had to know many investigations of this. I believe Nanto had more contacts and communicated more with the companies and was very pressured by the company ... they brought gifts and hatchets and machetes and other things. ... What possibility would ONHAE have, what possibility of helping the communities, what options could they have? And he signed the contract alone, in person. That was one of the problems that the old leaders had, they weren't together in one place.

Boya also reflected on Enquere's signing of the 1993 *convenio* with Maxus:

> I believe that we can no longer live with the companies. If it had been me in the time of Enquere, I would have made another form of work with the company, that they [the company] make more serious works. But Enquere, he got detoured from these things. And the company has the presence of the Huaorani leaders, they were always traveling, these Huaorani, to Quito, and the company was paying for good hotels so they could say they were working for the company.

During the same period in which this interview took place, of course, Maxus was paying for the ONHAE office and staff, and for Boya's frequent travel to the communities as well as to Quito. Money was also regularly received from Oryx, another oil company operating in Huaorani territory. This represents a fundamental problem in praxis for each successive generation of Huaorani leadership: while they oppose the oil companies, they have so far been unable to maintain a strong stand against them when the resources offered by the oil companies appear so great in the economic context of the Huaorani. Yet Boya was clear about his basic opposition to the oil companies:

Always my idea was to struggle. To defend my people and no more to permit the companies. Because I truly knew before, well, I do not want the companies, I knew how they destroyed, how they worked. Rachel [Saint] herself mentioned to us, she said "one day the company will destroy you all," even she said that to us. Well, many people have come and many have said "don't interfere more with us."

The making of separate agreements between ONHAE and the oil companies was seen by the leaders of other indigenous organizations as a serious breach of solidarity, and a threat to the negotiating positions of each of the other groups. As stated by Leonardo Viteri, an OPIP official and president of the Instituto Amazanga:

We have to establish mutual coordination between the indigenous peoples. There has been some weakening of interethnic relations more than anything because of the presence of the oil companies that have absolutely tried to separate us, to destroy the unity that we have forged in all of the region. That favors the company very much so they are able to get each group isolated and make agreements that favor the company.

In April of 1995 ONHAE took the radical step of mounting an armed occupation of Maxus oil drilling/pumping facilities in Huaorani territory. This "uprising" (*levantamiento*) was organized by Enquere and the ONHAE leadership with the cooperation and assistance of OPIP and CONFENIAE, and immediately received a great deal of international attention. However, the Huaorani involved in the occupation left after a few days. Moi explained to me that once they got tired of the food inside the encampment, they left to go hunting and to return to their families.

Leonardo Viteri, whose organization had supplied logistical and material aid to the action, is still bitter over the rapidity of the collapse of Huaorani resolve. He states:

It [the occupation] failed precisely—we had seen that the Huaorani people, being warriors, that know how to make decisions, on the other hand sometimes their positions become unstable, so they couldn't sustain the mobilization there. There was even an inter-ethnic negotiating team that had been formed, with substantial participation by the Huaorani, to get Maxus and the state to sit down at the negotiating table. But the company had its strategies too, and it knew the weak points of the Huaorani people. It immediately offered to make a deal. It offered to immediately make available certain resources in order to keep the work going. Under the circumstances the Huaorani failed to sustain their proposal for negotiations–they changed quickly. No more than two or three days passed. In that sense we felt a bit frustrated because we wanted the Huaorani to maintain their positions to the end.

Viteri and OPIP were not alone in their frustration. I spoke with representatives of several environmental groups based in both Quito and the U.S. All of them expressed frustration that after ONHAE and CONFENIAE had solicited their assistance, they had expended great effort in setting up the action and had then had to watch helplessly as the Huaorani quickly abandoned the struggle.

In 1994 ONHAE adopted its first formal set of by-laws, making the *Biye* itself the highest authority of the organization, able to set policy, elect and remove leaders, and approve agreements. It also established specific responsibilities for different vice presidents or secretaries.[5] These were initially drawn up with the help of OPIP and CONFENIAE and were later registered with the government as part of the process of legally creating the organization. This process of legal recognition, which in some ways strengthens the position of the organization, also establishes guidelines of conduct and prohibits certain activities: in effect, it forces an indigenous organization to adopt cultural and organizational forms that are alien to it. It also places its leaders and founders in some danger in the event that the government or some other entity wishes to crack down on the group. Conceivably, the leaders of a publicly recognized group could be punished for acts of resistance or rebellion conducted by the members of the group.

Another *Biye* was held in 1995, and Armando Boya Baihua, himself a resident of Toñampade, was elected president. Toca Caiga (also of Toñampade) was elected vice president for land; Nancy, the Daughter of Dayuma and wife of Delfin Andi (a Quichua schoolteacher in the Huaorani schools) and also a resident of Toñampade, was elected vice president for Health; and Gaba was elected vice president for education. These were the officers serving when I conducted this fieldwork.

Land Titling: A Great Success?

One of the first and greatest successes of the organization was the legalization of Huaorani territory, which took place just as the organization was being born in 1990. This government recognition, however, did not come without cost. When ONHAE was formed, one of its initial demands was the legalization of its territory. The traditional range of the Huaorani people included the area known as the "Protectorate" that had been controlled as a reservation by the Summer Institute of Linguistics prior to its expulsion. It also included a large unsettled central area and much of the Yasuní National Park. This park was designated by UNESCO as a "biosphere reserve," where oil exploration and extraction was prohibited. According to Thomson and Dudley (in Place 1993: 50-52), besides being home to the Huaorani, the Yasuní River drainage area is the "richest in the entire region, containing fifty species of fish, five hundred bird species and over one hundred mammal species, including jaguar, ocelot, giant otter, freshwater dolphins, and at least ten species of primates."

When ONHAE presented its territorial demands, the government of Ecuador, with great ceremony and remarkably little resistance, granted the Huaorani title to an area roughly the size of Puerto Rico, which represented a very large proportion of traditional lands and all of the known Huaorani communities. This transfer, made in April of 1990, gave the Huaorani the largest reserve of indigenous land in the country (see map). In making the territorial grant, the government carved out more than a third of the internationally recognized Yasuní National Park and transferred it to the Huaorani.

But there was a catch. When the transfer of title was made, the government simply retained all subsurface mineral rights, thereby making possible the exploitation of oil reserves in this area. Further, the government could award drilling, pipeline, and extraction permits without giving anything back to the Huaorani. As in most of the capitalist legal systems in the world, mineral rights may be sold independent of the land itself, and the owner of the mineral rights may not be impeded in efforts to extract the minerals. Immediately after granting the Huaorani the territory, the Ecuadorian government divided the area into numbered "Blocks" and auctioned these blocks to the highest bidder. Under this arrangement, any attempt by the Huaorani to extract concessions from the oil companies operating in their territory or to impose a moratorium or an end to oil exploitation altogether, must rely on the moral force of their argument, for under settled rules of Ecuadorian and international law, they have no right or legal standing to interfere in the systematic alteration and destruction of their land caused by the extraction of oil.

By transferring the lands of the park in this manner the government had avoided much of the criticism that would have accompanied other means of permitting the oil development of Yasuní National Park. The government was able to claim that this transfer was occurring because of its concern and respect for indigenous rights, not primarily to provide for the exploitation of the oil reserves.

In spite of this loss of control over mineral rights and oil exploration, the maintenance of territorial integrity has been one of the highest priorities and greatest successes of ONHAE. They are in the midst of a difficult, multi-year process of marking the territorial boundaries by planting a border of a particular type of palm tree.[6] This physical marking of the territory is the best way to keep out the *colonos,* whose settlements and ranches are always getting closer to Huaorani land.

ONHAE 1996

By the time of this fieldwork, ONHAE was already established in an office with a fax machine, telephone service, and two non-Huaorani office support personnel. The officers spent much of their time in the office, whenever they were not on trips into the communities or to Quito. The office itself served a variety of purposes, both formal and informal, which will be discussed below.

It is important to understand a number of elements of the daily practice of the leadership of ONHAE in order to place their subsequent actions (such as the oil company agreements) in perspective. Even the comparatively worldly cadre of young literate men who make up the bulk of the Huaorani leadership are completely new to such basic elements of organizational administration as bank accounts, rent, loans, interest, salary, and taxes. Such skills as telephone etiquette, the use of office machines, and much more are things that must be learned. More complex duties, like grant applications and detailed accounting, for example, require continuous assistance. The leadership of ONHAE has therefore hired a number of non-Huaorani to act as office help. This was done with the assistance of Maxus, and has left these *mestiza* employees, who retain their ties to Maxus, in charge of the organization's funds, files, documents, and records. At the same time the employment relationship has inverted much of the traditional relationship between "*indio*" and "*mestizo*" in terms of status, power, and familiarity. Moreover, the daily experience of the ONHAE leadership is not the life of a Huaorani community. During their term of office the leaders live in Puyo-Shell, and the physical spaces and personal relationships that surround them represent the contextual background of actual praxis. How the office spaces are divided, how time spent in the office is used, and relations with present and past leaders as well as Huaorani and non-Huaorani visitors are all reflected in the utilization of space in the office environment.

The city of Puyo is the administrative and transportation center of the *oriente* (eastern jungle) province of Pastaza. It has a population of approximately 16,000 and is growing rapidly. It has two major markets, a wide variety of stores and restaurants, several schools, and most of the area's meager entertainment attractions. A large Roman Catholic church dominates what was probably intended to be the town's central square, but development has made this a more out-of-the-way place than originally intended. In addition, there are a number of small "storefront" evangelical churches. The offices of OPIP and the Instituto Amazanga are found in central Puyo. Puyo is also where Moi maintains a small home.

A fifteen-minute bus ride takes one from Puyo to the much smaller town of Shell,[7] dominated by a large military base with a shared-use (civilian/military) airstrip and a large fenced compound for North American missionaries. This compound contains field offices for all of the missionary activities in the *oriente*, residences for many of the missionaries, and a school (named for Nathan

Saint) for the children of missionaries. Shell is also the home of the missionary-run Hospital Vozandes, largely staffed by North American evangelical volunteers. In addition, Shell has a variety of general stores, restaurants, and brothels, largely geared toward the military personnel.

Shell is where ONHAE has its office and where the officers and leaders share a house. Located a short walk from the main road through Shell, the house is a typical small cement dwelling, only sparsely furnished. During Boya's administration all of the officers lived there, and Huaorani visitors to Puyo/Shell frequently stayed there as well. Other than myself, I never knew of any non-Huaorani visitors staying in the house. The house is just a few blocks from the office, making it easy for the officers to stop in at the office at odd times, and to come in to the office for the nightly radio service to the communities or to use the telephone.

The office of ONHAE is located in what was built as a second-floor apartment above a small store in Shell. The letters "ONHAE" are carefully stenciled in large letters on the uppermost wall of the house facing toward the main street of Shell, which is the same road that normally connects Puyo with Baños.[8] One enters the office via an outside staircase and through an unmarked door. Once inside the entry hall, there are several separate offices—one private office for the president, one for Clara, the *mestiza* bookkeeper, and one which I shared with a *mestiza* secretary/receptionist named Rocio. There is also a room used as a combination office and storage locker by Nancy, the vice president for health, and a disused kitchen filled with cast-off articles as well as equipment used in periodic expeditions to mark the boundaries of Huaorani territory ("*linderación*"). Beyond these rooms are a small bathroom and a large meeting room approximately 15 by 40 feet. The meeting room has a few tables and chairs, an old typewriter, and some maps of Ecuador and of Huaorani territory. This large room is used by Moi when he is visiting, and for large meetings, particularly between ONHAE officials and representatives of Maxus' Department of Community Relations. The office has two balconies—one in front, which is accessed from the main hallway and communicates with the President's office and the bookkeeper's, and another smaller one in the rear, which is entered from the large room. The cement building is a typical example of local vernacular architecture and, like many such buildings in Latin America, is always under construction. Steel reinforcing rods jut out from the top walls, and the stairway continues beyond the level of the roof, promising the eventual construction of a third floor. The parquet floors are hand cut from local hardwoods and are quite beautiful although very worn. The interior of the office is spartan, almost completely without decoration, and badly in need of a fresh coat of paint. There are several more or less modern steel desks and filing cabinets, which I was told were gifts from Maxus, a few cheap office chairs, and a miscellany of mismatched tables, chairs, and other household items from sources unknown.

Nancy's office also holds the radio that enables communication with most of the Huaorani communities. When Smith (1993: 266-77) conducted his census of the Huaorani communities, he found that only six communities had radios. By the time of my fieldwork, twelve of the eighteen communities had radios. The radio frequency was shared by ONHAE and the missionary compound, and ONHAE was authorized to use the radios only between six and eight P.M. Each evening some of the officers would gather in the radio room and listen for messages from the communities. In the forest, the radios are powered by solar-charged batteries, which often do not have enough power on cloudy days. Nevertheless, the radio provides the most frequent communication between ONHAE and the various Huaorani communities. News of births, deaths, and illnesses, the activities of the oil company workers, and ONHAE's activities is passed by means of the radio. The radio may be playing an important role in the development of a "Huaorani consciousness" or sense of a larger group identity that extends beyond one's own *nanicabo* or community. Everyone hears the news from each of the other Huaorani communities, and thus contact of a sort is always maintained between these communities and ONHAE, Puyo, and the broader world. As an example, Boya and Toca used the radio constantly to mobilize forest dwelling Huaorani to come out and support Pachakutik by voting in the national elections in July and to organize the delegations for the *Biye*. It has also had the effect of giving the Huaorani leadership at least some centralized control over the flow of information; Moi, for example, was not able to use the radio when he was trying to influence the selection of delegates for the *Biye* in order to be able to mount a challenge to Boya's leadership.

In addition to the officers of ONHAE, the two regular full-time office support staff mentioned above were employed throughout my fieldwork. Both worked regular full-time hours and were frequently left in charge of the office for days or even weeks at a time while the officers of ONHAE were in Huaorani territory or in Quito. They were paid partly by Maxus and partly through a grant from the Ibis Foundation of Denmark.

The first of the employees was Rocio Toscano, the office secretary and receptionist. Rocio was a *mestiza* single mother in her late twenties from Puyo who had completed *colegio* (high school) in Puyo as well as a secretarial training course. She clearly did not come to the organization as an ideologically motivated ONHAE supporter, although she subsequently indicated on a number of occasions that she has come to have an interest in supporting ONHAE and the Huaorani. Rocio was responsible for handling all incoming and outgoing correspondence (including faxes), maintaining the nonfinancial files, answering the telephone, greeting visitors, and generally keeping the office operating on a regular basis. She spoke often with Milton Ortega from Maxus, and sometimes had lunch with him and others from Maxus' department of "community relations." She explained that she had originally been hired by Maxus for the job.

The other regular non-Huaorani employee was Clara Beccara, the bookkeeper. Also a *mestiza*, Clara had taken courses locally in basic bookkeeping procedures. She worked full-time, with her own office and files, handling all of the banking, accounts, payroll, and other financial matters. I observed that she was frequently on the telephone with representatives of both Maxus and Oryx (another of the international oil companies presently operating in Huaorani territory).

The daily routine in the office began between 8:30 and 9:00 A.M. when Rocio and Clara arrived and opened the office. Both traveled from Puyo by a public bus that left from the center of Puyo and stopped directly in front of the ONHAE office in Shell. They generally followed what could be called "standard office practice." They remained at the office until about 4:30 or 5:00 P.M. and usually spent most of their time at their desks working. They took lunch, usually together, in one of several small restaurants serving a fixed price *almuerzo* right in Shell. With some frequency one or the other would take afternoons off to attend to personal business, a practice that is very common throughout Ecuador. In conversations, they both mentioned having gotten their jobs through Maxus, but both vehemently denied that they were actually Maxus employees.

In addition to Clara and Rocio, a third woman, Lucia Palacio, was working at the office when I did my preliminary fieldwork in 1995. She openly stated that she was a Maxus employee from Quito and the wife of a career army officer who had been transferred to the Shell base. She said that it had been an "internal transfer" for her to come from the Quito office of Maxus to ONHAE. When I returned in 1996 she was no longer working with ONHAE; Rocio Toscano and Armando Boya both said that she had only stayed "a few months."

There was also an Ecuadorian soldier who came in several times to "work with" the Huaorani. He stopped in about once every two weeks, looked at private correspondence, questioned me extensively ("What are you doing here? What do you want to find out? How long will you be here?"). When he saw that I had brought a computer, he wanted to know what it could do, and wanted to know all about e-mail, at one point trying to get me to tell him my password. His visits appear more sinister when one factors in that after I had finished my work and left, he came in (within weeks) and offered to help with the computer. In the process of "helping" he erased all of the software from the computer and uninstalled the modem. I was never able to obtain more information about him, but it seems likely that he was sent by some combination of the Army, Petroecuador, and the Ecuadorian government to keep tabs on the Huaorani organization.

Another regular presence in the office was an unmarried Huao woman, Manuela Ima, who came in every day to clean the office and run errands for the officers and staff. She was referred to as the *conserje*, which I discovered later was an elected office in ONHAE, and lived in the house in Shell with the rest of the elected officials.

There she also did the cooking and food shopping for the group—in a sense replicating some of the relationships and responsibilities of *nanicabo* life.

In addition to the officers and employees of ONHAE (and myself), there was a steady stream of visitors. These visitors represented a wide range of interests and attitudes, and reflect the different forces swirling about the leadership of ONHAE.

Representatives of Maxus visited every week to ten days and averaged two telephone calls per day and two faxes per week. They were greeted warmly by the paid staff and by Boya, who called Milton Ortega "*hermano*" regularly, and they met with Boya in his office or (occasionally) in the large meeting room. These were private meetings, and the only such meetings at which great pains were taken to maintain that privacy—doors were closed, windows were closed and locked, and the meeting participants spoke in whispers. This secrecy and cooperation was particularly evident following the *Biye*, as will be discussed in the next chapter. The oil company representatives made themselves very much at home when they visited. When they first met me, I was questioned extensively about my research, how long I would be staying, and what I was doing. It was common for them to sit down with Clara and go over the ONHAE financial and bank records. On one occasion, after I had helped Clara to computerize a number of bookkeeping functions, she asked me to print out a transaction record so that Milton Ortega could take it with him. At no time did I see any behavior by either Huaorani leaders or Maxus representatives that could be described as confrontational or hostile.

Huaorani visiting Puyo-Shell from their communities were the next most frequent group of visitors. For most Huaorani a trip to town is a rare event involving tremendous effort or the serendipitous opportunity to hitch a ride on a missionary or tourist plane. Many who came were visiting in order to receive medical treatment at the Hospital Vozandes in Shell. These visits were frequently prolonged by the hospital's refusal, for most of the time of my fieldwork, to treat any noncritical cases without payment in advance. Individuals who were clearly very ill sometimes had to wait weeks for ONHAE or some family member to provide them with funds.[9] In one case, a woman from Quehueire Ono lay on the floor of my office by day and on my sofa by night, in obvious pain, until I finally went with her to the hospital and paid the approximately $6 for her to receive treatment. Others came to Puyo just to explore or to spend money they had received from sales to tourists or from work performed for the oil companies. Once they got to Puyo-Shell, many of the Huaorani stayed with Boya and some of the other officers in Shell or with Moi in Puyo, or with me. During the day, they frequently came into the ONHAE office and sat, told stories, and joked with one another and with the officers. Sometimes they would be fixtures in the office for weeks. One man, Pancho, from Toñampade, stayed for more than a month and spent most of his days in the ONHAE office. Partly, this presence in the office was related to the fact that ONHAE usually knew if there was anyone flying into any of the communities, so they could arrange for someone to "hitch a ride" back home. Most of the visiting Huaorani came from the more acculturated upriver communities, where outside (missionary) influence is strongest–places like Toñampade, Kiwado, Tihueno, and Quehueire Ono. Only on rare occasions did anyone from the Yasuní or Cononaco groups make it to Shell, and then it was usually due to a medical emergency.

A third, surprisingly common category of visitor, was the European or North American would-be environmentalist. During my fieldwork no fewer than seventeen such visitors appeared at the ONHAE office. They were from Denmark, Sweden, England, Spain, and Canada. In some cases these people would show up claiming to be journalists or scientists; in fact, they were usually low-budget ecotourists. The ONHAE officers were always cordial to such visitors and would freely give them the written permission needed to enter Huaorani territory. I spoke at length with a number of these visitors, and none of them reported being asked (directly or obliquely) for any money or payment for the *permiso*; some, however, were asked for money by individuals (including Moi) who offered their services as guides. In addition, they usually offered to treat Boya and other officers to a meal or two. The presence of these visitors was referred to frequently by Moi, Boya, and Enquere, who cited their interest in the Huaorani to demonstrate the importance of the Huaorani in the greater world. Moi, in particular, had his anti-oil, environmentalist views reinforced by his frequent conversations with these tourists. It should be mentioned that most of the arriving tourists had read Joe Kane's 1995 book or his 1993 New Yorker article and already saw Moi as something of a celebrity. They were frequently less interested in Boya and the other contemporary officers.

On one occasion in particular, Moi used a pair of Danish tourists very effectively to "finance" a campaign trip to a number of different communities. He offered his services as a guide for free if the pair would pay for him (and me) to accompany them. The trip included more than six separate Huaorani communities and took more than three weeks. When Moi arrived in each community, he began by distributing a variety of small gifts (purchased by his Danish charges) and then conducted what could only be called a campaign rally, at which he denounced the present leadership of ONHAE, especially Boya, as being under the control of the oil companies. He answered questions and urged everyone to attend the upcoming *Biye.* Although I never heard him announce publicly that he was going to try to unseat and replace Boya, he confided in me that that was his plan. He was well received in every community we visited, and in each place people came to seek his help with problems they were experiencing. This led me to believe that he had a sufficient following to at least mount a credible challenge to Boya's leadership. As will be discussed in the following chapter, this turned out to be a complete misjudgment.

Surprisingly, there were very few missionaries visiting the office of ONHAE, although the central missionary compound for the *oriente,* the missionary aviation terminal, and the missionary hospital are all within a few blocks of the office. Stephan Saint came to the office once, and messengers delivered papers from the missionaries on occasion, but when meetings were required Boya always went to the missionary compound for them. Generally, the missionaries were not friendly to ONHAE and in private were highly critical of both its leadership and its mission. In private, I heard missionaries denounce ONHAE and its leaders as "communists;" one missionary spoke of her sadness that all of the activists and officials had "strayed" and were "agents of the devil."

According to both Boya and Moi, Rachel Saint (who was still alive and active during the early years of ONHAE's existence) initially claimed to support the idea of creating a representative organization, but quickly changed her view. They all recognized that it was Rachel Saint who had actively encouraged the oil companies, particularly Maxus, whose president William Hutton professes to be an evangelical Christian.

My only opportunity to interview Stephan Saint came when he visited the office. He became particularly vehement in his denunciation of ONHAE when he said that the organization did not represent the Huaorani people and that by its nature it excluded the older generations that did not speak Spanish. He further stated that the leaders were changed by their contact with outsiders and that they were no longer a part of the "tribal life" and no longer wanted to be. He stated that they had been influenced by leftists and had abandoned traditional Huao values. Stephan also actively discouraged Huaorani from participating in ONHAE activities (including the *Biye*) and apparently tried to sabotage ONHAE's efforts to organize and to be more inclusive (see Chapter 3).

Only occasionally did representatives of other indigenous organizations visit the ONHAE offices. When meetings were scheduled between leaders of ONHAE and representatives of OPIP, Instituto Amazanga, or CONFENIAE, they took place in the offices of OPIP (in Puyo) or at one of several "better" restaurants (particularly the Meson Europeo).

The officers themselves seemed to work very differently in the office. Armando Boya spent between 10 and 20 hours per week in the office, more than any other Huaorani officer, although he also was constantly traveling to different communities and to Quito. Boya always had a large number of telephone messages, usually including several calls from Maxus. There were also frequent calls and faxes from OPIP and CONFENIAE, as well as from representatives of one of the several Ecuador-based environmental groups.[10] Boya did not pay much attention to the financial condition of the organization, and on several occasions asked Clara to write checks for which there were not sufficient funds. Clara told me that at no time did he ever inspect the books or even inquire as to the bank account balances.

Toca Caigo, the vice president for land, was in the office almost as much as Boya, but frequently was not engaged in any sort of

ONHAE activity. He was often just relaxing and gossiping. He was also left "in charge" of the office whenever Boya was to be out of town for any length of time. Although he spoke frequently of the work involved in "*linderación*," the process of marking the limits of legalized Huaorani territory by planting a border of palm trees, he never took concrete steps to organize such a project during his tenure, which became the primary reason for his being replaced at the 1996 *Biye*.

Nancy, the vice-president for health, was in the office one or two days per week (on average) for a few hours. Nancy was at the time of fieldwork the only female elected officer of the organization. She is a woman of considerable status, being the daughter of Dayuma and the wife of a Quichua schoolteacher. Her Quichua husband, Delfin Andy, was in the office three or four days per week, usually all day. The bulk of his time in the office was spent working on various projects for ONHAE, including a newsletter, teacher training and recruitment, and drafting rules for tour guides to follow in Huaorani territory. He made a point of identifying his children as Huaorani and he expressed a real sense of solidarity with the Huaorani when he stated:

> I have been a teacher in the Huaorani schools for twelve years. My only aspiration is to live my life in the Huaorani sector and to see the Huaorani organized, not by me but by themselves. So that they think for themselves and analyze for themselves, not that they look to some-one outside to give them aid [*asilo*] whether it's the missionaries or the oil companies. That is why I have involved myself in this great challenge. If I teach my students but then everything is the same as before then that's no good—if I teach them, it's so that they can overcome. That's why I've been working with the Huaorani leaders from the beginning. ... I feel part of the Huaorani people.

Relations with the other indigenous organizations (OPIP, CONFENIAE, Amazanga, and others) were cordial but frequently strained. The occupation, discussed above, left many of the leaders of OPIP and CONFENIAE angry at ONHAE because they had invested a great deal of time and energy helping ONHAE to organize the occupation, only to have the Huaorani abandon the project after two and a half days. There were also frequent disputes over money that ONHAE was said to owe to OPIP for the use of the AEROPIP plane. The ONHAE leaders had an arrangement with OPIP whereby the Huaorani could use the OPIP plane for trips to the communities and ONHAE would pay part of the maintenance and repair costs for the plane's operation. While I was working in the office there was a very angry exchange between Hector Villamil[11] (then president of OPIP) and Boya because Boya had not paid ONHAE's share when the plane had required a new motor.

It is worth noting that following his term as president of ONHAE (and subsequent to my fieldwork), Boya became a vice president of CONFENIAE, the first Huaorani to hold such a post. His involvement with CONFENIAE had intensified (during the period of my fieldwork) when the national election process began. In 1996, for the first time ever, the indigenous federations formed a political party–Pachakutik/Nuevo Pais, whose presidential candidate finished third nationally in a field of almost twenty candidates– and elected a sizable block of national legislators. Boya and Toca worked hard to bring Huaorani from the different communities into town to vote, and all of the leaders spent a great deal of time working with the local Pachakutik leadership (in one week Boya spent more than thirty hours in the Puyo headquarters of the party). This exposure seemed to influence their conception of a pan-indigenous movement and brought the leadership into more constant and familiar contact with the leaders of CONFENIAE and CONAIE. It is too early to tell if this will have any lasting effect on the structure or behavior of ONHAE's leadership elements.

Boya's frequent trips to the communities were all motivated by ONHAE business, but the number of hours of "work" on these trips was often less important than the politicking that went on. For example, I accompanied Boya on a trip to Tihueno, Quenahueno, and Toñampade at Easter time in 1996. On this trip, which lasted for seven days, he held meetings in Tihueno and Quenahueno, reporting to residents there about ONHAE's work and introducing me to each of the community members. However, the trip to Toñampade appeared to be a pleasure trip: he spent virtually all of his time in the three-house compound of his extended family. Of course part of what he was doing was similar to what American politicians do on a home state visit, drinking *tepe* and giving away rice instead of kissing babies and giving away Thanksgiving turkeys. One of the things that I realized was that a great deal of active political maneuvering goes on within ONHAE's leadership. Suggestions that the Huaorani leadership does not feel responsible for the entire nation are seriously mistaken. While there may be naïveté concerning some aspects of their dealings with the outside world of contracts, governments, and multinational oil companies, the current generation of ONHAE leaders understands the importance of politics in the acquisition and maintenance of political power through the organization.

Further, I believe that the traditional Huao practice of reciprocity, usually restricted to one's own *nanicabo*, has been carried over by at least some Huaorani leaders to a sense of responsibility to provide benefits and contribute to each and every community. Thus the strong desire on the part of Huaorani leaders to provide bags of rice and other bulk foods to communities, to see schools built, airstrips expanded, and medical needs met. These are all positive contributions for which the incumbent leadership can take credit. I have heard Milton Ortega, the head of Maxus' department of "community relations" use such an argument while cajoling the president of ONHAE to take gifts from the company to the communities.

Specifically, when Boya and I arrived at a community, the first thing he would do after getting us established in a household was to call everyone together and distribute gifts like combs, shotgun shells, canned tuna, and (if we were arriving by air) rice. He would take credit for bringing these things to the community and remind the recipients of any recently completed project that might have had even the most minor sponsorship of ONHAE, such as the school building and new teacher in Tihueno. Only following this distribution of goods would any kind of discussion or meeting begin. It is also worth noting that he always presented me to these meetings as another of his accomplishments–a *cowode* working for ONHAE and helping the Huaorani. I believe Maxus has taken advantage of the leaders' perceived need to provide food and goods for each of the communities as if they were somehow extensions of their own *nanicabos*. The company provides cheap goods that the president or other ONHAE official can then take credit for. Contracts, "convenios," and other agreements frequently do not seem as real or as serious to the Huaorani as tangible artifacts and food. Boya (who has also signed agreements with the oil companies) told me that "if we don't want [oil exploitation] to continue we will reject the contract with the company." Enquere had also stated that the continuation of the contract he signed with Maxus and Petroecuador will depend

> on the behavior of the oil company—it was declared in front of the President of the Republic who was present at the meeting. If the oil company behaves badly we will reject the contract. But the [government representative] said that if Maxus behaves badly we should speak first with the President of the Republic! (laughs)

What the company has also done is to establish very personalized relationships between Boya (and previously Enquere and Nanto) and the Maxus "community relations" specialists. Boya has said that when he receives things from Milton Ortega, he feels "obligated" to do something for him. Maxus has also been able to establish a certain amount of organizational dependency. The company pays for the ONHAE office. They have provided much of the furniture and office machines for the office. They pay part of the salaries of the office staff and were instrumental in hiring and training them. Oryx (another oil company) has also been making payments to ONHAE. These payments are not personal "bribes," but I believe that they have had the effect of creating a sense of obligation on the part of the Huaorani leaders.

Boya, despite working closely with Maxus and Oryx, has repeatedly stated his opposition to the Oil companies' presence in Huaorani territory.

> Many things made me start to think. When Exxon put wells very near Toñampade, just four kilometers away they put wells, and they manipulated us. ... we knew what was going to happen, with this work they were going to do, more companies were going to come. That's why the Huaorani said no. We don't have to expand the airstrip, and we said, "what will happen with these companies," and most people—the old people—said no. The companies have not respected us. When they come, they destroy.

The stated policy of ONHAE at the time of my fieldwork, reinforced by a series of similarly worded *Biye* resolutions, was that there should be a complete moratorium (*moratorio*) on oil development in the territory. However, in the same breath the leaders would add that Maxus had to live up to the *convenio* and that it was all right for ONHAE to receive money from Oryx and other assistance from Petroecuador. As will be shown in the next chapter, even resolutions made by the *Biye* were altered or ignored by the leadership of the organization under pressure from the oil companies, particularly Maxus.

The ONHAE office functioned somewhat effectively as an advocate for Huaorani education, land rights, and health care, areas in which there was no concerted opposition to confront. At the time of this fieldwork the organization was beginning to look for a role in economic development and tourism projects. ONHAE was instrumental in generating a pan-Huaorani identity and consciousness. However, the organization consistently failed to maintain its position in reference to the oil operations being commenced in their territory. They were placated by comparatively small gifts and aid from the companies involved. The organization was not capable of confronting an entity with the resources, sophistication, and determination of a large multinational capitalist enterprise.

Notes

1. A *Biye* (as will be detailed in Chapter 3) is a large group meeting of representatives of different Huaorani communities.
2. Besides being an acronym, ONHAE means flower in Huao Terero.
3. Confederación de las Nacionalidades Indígena de la Amazonia Ecuatoriana, the regional Indian federation; Confederación de las Nacionalidades Indígenas Ecuatorianas, the national indigenous federation; and the Organización de los Pueblos Indígenas de Pastaza, the Quichua-dominated provincial federation.
4. Throughout this work I will use the Spanish word *convenio* to refer to the agreement between Maxus and ONHAE. This agreement is not a "contract" as it is not legally enforceable, but it is frequently treated as a contract by the company and its representatives.

5. The by-laws call the persons responsible for land, health, etc. "Secretary", but in practice Nancy and Toca referred to themselves and are referred to by others as Vice presidents.

6. For a good account of this process by a participant see Smith 1993.

7. "Shell" was originally constructed as the regional base for oil exploration by Royal Dutch Shell during the 1930s and 40s.

8. Throughout the period in which this fieldwork was conducted, the road to Baños was closed for major reconstruction, a situation that wrought economic havoc in Shell and to a lesser extent in Puyo.

9. The hospital officials (U.S. missionaries) claimed that ONHAE owed them money for treatment that they had performed in the past, but my discussions with doctors and nurses at the hospital revealed a much deeper animosity toward ONHAE. One nurse told me in a whisper that although the Huaorani generally were like children, those involved with the organization were both "crazy" and "communists".

10. Rainforest Information Center (RIC), Acción Ecologica, and the OPIP-affiliated Instituto Amazanga.

11. Villamil was later elected *diputado* to the Ecuadorian House of Deputies as a member of Pachakutik. While in office, he allied himself with President Abdala Bucaram and was subsequently accused of corruption and driven from office.

Chapter 3

PRACTICE AND PRAXIS
ONHAE in Action

As was previously discussed, ONHAE, like all activist organi-zations constructed on the basis of a particular racial, ethnic, or cultural group (ethnic entrepreneurship), must operate simulta-neously within and across different social/cultural spheres. As a representative organization, its leaders must receive validation from and maintain the respect of the Huaorani community itself in order to preserve the organization's credibility. At the same time, the central focus of the organization's founding was to create an intermediary entity–one that could represent the Huaorani people effectively in the context of national (and international) society. In both of these realms respect for the organization and its leaders is indispensable in maintaining the effectiveness of the group. Over the relatively short history of the organization, ONHAE has devel-oped practices or patterns of behavior and engagement which have allowed the leaders to build and maintain these relationships. In turn, these relationships are critical to the continued reproduction of ONHAE through time.

The regular practice of the ONHAE office and some of the routine activities of the leadership have already been described.

Notes for this section can be found on page 139.

This chapter will explore two specific events: one from the "internal" sphere (within Huaorani society) discussed above, and the other representative of the multifaceted interactions between ONHAE, the Huaorani people, and the mestizo-dominated national culture of Ecuador.

Part One: *Biye* 1996

Much of what has been discussed concerning the Huaorani in general and ONHAE in particular can be illustrated by a careful study of the *Biye* of 1996 and the events surrounding it. As part of my fieldwork I was able to observe and participate in the planning of the event, and I was privy to the details of funding, logistics, agenda, and the internal disagreements leading up to the event itself. I was able to participate in the *Biye* itself, and to speak at length to the participants during the event as well as after. Finally, I was able to observe what became of the resolutions passed by the *Biye* in the subsequent conferences with Maxus representatives.

The *Biye* is the annual meeting of Huaorani representatives from all of the communities. According to the ONHAE by-laws, the *Biye* is the supreme authority governing all ONHAE policy. It has been rationalized and contextualized by the claim that it is a traditional form of meeting from before contact and missionization. However, none of the older Huaorani that I asked remembered any event resembling a modern *Biye*. Instead, several of the older men described meetings with neighboring or closely related *nanicabos* to discuss marriages, and said that the word *Biye* came from these marriage conferences. In any event, the *Biye* has become the primary event in the regular functioning of ONHAE and the principal method of communication between the ONHAE leadership cadre and the "rank-and-file" membership population of the communities.

The 1996 *Biye* serves as a case study of several important factors. First, it highlights the political interplay between and among the leadership cadre, their relationships with the communities, and the relationships between genders, generations, and evangelical and non-evangelical Huaorani. A second factor is the relations the organization and its leadership maintain with the oil companies, missionaries, environmentalists, and others. And finally, it demonstrates the ability of a geographically and politically fragmented group to adopt in a limited manner the forms and ideologies of "representative democracy" and the syncretic relationship between traditional and alien methods of group decision making and organization.

The Planning Stages

At the start of my fieldwork, when I was still in the process of becoming acclimated to the ONHAE office and leadership, I heard about the *asemblea*, and the *congreso*, and the *Biye*. When I asked I was first told that these were three different types of meetings, something I later discovered was simply not true in practice. I was disappointed when I was initially told that in 1996 there was to be no *Biye*, but I soon learned that there had been a *Biye* every year since the founding of the organization and that there would certainly be one this year.

The first time I heard about the 1996 *Biye* was when Moi, while visiting Puyo in late January, began to talk about the "upcoming *Biye*" with Boya. Soon Boya began talking about the *Biye*, and how it was to be arranged, where it was to be held, and so on. Although Boya and Moi saw each other almost every day, both in and out of the office, it soon became clear that they were describing the upcoming *Biye* in very different terms. Throughout February and early March, Moi stated repeatedly that the *Biye* would be held in his home community of Quehueire Ono, while Boya was equally clear that it would take place in Toñampade. When I spoke with Boya in private, he dismissed Moi's claims, saying that he was president and he alone could decide where and when the *Biye* would take place. He also stated that since his term was not up there was no way he would be replaced and that there would not even be an election of officers; instead, the *Biye* would be exclusively to discuss issues and pass resolutions setting policy for the organization. Despite Boya's private declarations, when the two were together in the office during this period they were invariably friendly and sometimes socialized together outside of the office. It is worth noting, however, that Moi always maintained his own house in Puyo at considerable expense and sacrifice, and did not stay in the house where the leadership lived, although there was ample space (by Huaorani standards) and it was common practice for Huaorani visitors to Puyo-Shell to stay with the leaders. There was never any sign of open hostility between them, which is very much in keeping with what I observed of Huaorani interpersonal relationships: anger is generally not demonstrated until it is about to erupt into something with the potential for violence.

The dispute over the location of the *Biye* was something that was likely to directly impact the results of the meetings. Delegates to the *Biye* are chosen from each community, but this is not strictly related to population. In organizing the *Biye*, Boya decided how many flights would go to each community to pick up delegates, and that was generally what determined how many could come from a given community. Anyone else who wished to participate in the *Biye* seemed to be able to do so–certainly quite a few of the residents of Toñampade attended the *Biye*, participated, and voted without any apparent "selection" process having taken place. Thus a *Biye* in a candidate's own home community is likely to favor that candidate. Quehueire Ono is Moi's home community; had the meetings been held there, Moi would presumably have been able to count on the support of his extended kin network as well as his and his family's friends. Additionally, Quehueire Ono has a reputation for stridency and for favoring comparatively more radical solutions. Not coincidentally, it is also the one Huaorani settlement that has more or less explicitly rejected the missionary presence and embraced Mengotohue, the last true Huaorani shaman. Boya's home community of Toñampade, which had been Rachel Saint's home until her death, was where his extended kin network lived and where support for him would be greatest. Having the meetings in Toñampade would also allow Boya to act as host for the event, and to bring delegates whose support might be wavering to his house there as guests.

By the end of February Moi was actively campaigning to replace Boya, and in the first week of March Moi left (with me and the two Danish tourists mentioned earlier) to campaign in the communities as was discussed in the previous chapter. Moi's campaign was tacitly supported by many of the members of the environmentalist community in Ecuador; in a conversation I had with María from Acción Ecologica in Quito, she expressed her private hope that Moi would win since he had more of an "environmental conscience" than Boya. Andy Drumm, an environmentalist, university ecotourism professor, and owner of an ecotourism-oriented travel agency who has worked with the Huaorani for many years, actively supported and advised Moi on his campaign. His was typical of the support Moi garnered among environmentalists and other progressive forces. As far as I know, Moi was not receiving money or other material aid from these individuals within Ecuador; rather, they provided moral support and encouragement, telling Moi that he was a star and that he should run and win. Moi did claim to have received money for his campaign from author Joe Kane and from the Rainforest Action Network; however, this seems unlikely. If he did receive any money from Joe Kane, it would have been some of the royalties from his 1995 book which he frequently sent to Moi to help support him and his environmental work, not as a campaign contribution, although this is a very tenuous distinction in this context. Of course, none of these non-Huaorani supporters knew much about the internal politics of the Huaorani communities.

At the same time that Moi's campaign was beginning, Boya told me that the meetings were definitely going to be held in late April or early May, either in Toñampade or in Quihuaro. I asked him about the possibility of the meetings taking place in Quehueire Ono and he told me that he had argued ("chocó") with Moi about where the meetings should be, but that he was president and therefore he could decide where they were to be. Boya was working a great many hours in this period. He was constantly on the telephone trying to arrange flights with AEROPIP, private charter companies, and Alas de Socorro, the missionary air service and a pseudonym for the Missionary Aviation Fellowship (MAF). The dates for the *Biye* were largely determined by the availability of the air services, and the choice of where to hold the event was influenced by what the pilots felt were the runways best suited to accommodate such a large volume of air traffic. The fact that the largest single group of civilian planes in the region belongs to the missionaries gave the evangelicals a great deal of control over ONHAE's ability to meet. They did not seem to use this power to prevent the meeting, and they did provide the planes for the *Biye*, but it should be noted that the missionaries, through their air service, have the (as yet unrealized) power to seriously impede ONHAE's ability to function.[1]

Boya, together with Toca and the pilots from Alas de Socorro, finally decided to have the *Biye* at Toñampade beginning on 27 April. Earlier discussions had involved other dates, all of them much earlier; some of the original suggested dates were in late February or early March. This would have been preferable because the rainy season begins in April frequently making the dirt landing strips in the jungle unusable.

I had a number of conversations with both Boya and Moi at this time. They seemed to have completely contradictory understandings of what was to take place at the meetings. Moi told me that he was going to be able to replace Boya and that Boya had agreed not to fight to keep his position. Moi also stated to me on 13 March that he (Moi) had been asked to arrange the meeting. Boya, on the other hand, said that there would not even be elections for new officers because his full term had not yet expired, and that this *Biye* was intended only to discuss issues and set policy for the organization.

For an organization such as ONHAE a *Biye* is an expensive undertaking. Each flight costs between $60 and $100, and the delegates expect to be fed, and fed well, throughout the meeting. Also, a special meeting house is usually constructed, a huge version of a traditional Huao house, and this construction must be paid for as well. At first, Boya sought funding for the *Biye* from Maxus, which had paid the expenses of such gatherings in the past. But a number of environmental activists, including representatives of Acción Ecologica, the Rainforest Information Center, and Leonardo Viteri and other representatives of OPIP, urged Boya to find some other way to fund the meetings. Through the intervention of Andy Drumm and Joe Kane (who has been affiliated with the Rainforest Action Network in the United States), it was finally arranged that the Rainforest Action Network (RAN) would pay for the costs of the *Biye*. They provided a grant of several thousand dollars, which they sent through Andy Drumm in Quito. At first Boya wanted to take the money from RAN and still take money from Maxus and invite Maxus representatives to the *Biye*. Only when Andy Drumm and I suggested that Maxus representatives could influence the *Biye* did Boya decide not to invite them to the meeting. Boya called Milton Ortega at Maxus and told him very apologetically that he would not be receiving an invitation. During that telephone call he also set up a meeting with Ortega for the day following the *Biye* to discuss the resolutions decided upon. Boya then stated that no *cowode* would be invited to the meetings, but he changed that the next day to say that I could come. Later, invitations were sent to a few government officials and to the military commander of the Shell base, but none of these individuals attended. Rocio, Clara, and I were the only non Huaorani to attend the *Biye* in 1996.

As the *Biye* approached, much of the conversation among the leaders of ONHAE was about food and the feasting that would take place at the *Biye*. Those whose homes were in Toñampade or who had relatives there all invited me to stay in their homes, promising me that there would be great food and plenty of *tepe*. In the end I decided to stay with Nancy, partly to avoid being linked too directly to either Boya or Moi and partly because it would give me the opportunity to speak regularly with Dayuma, whose role in the community and personal history give her a unique perspective on the proceedings.

The Biye

The *Biye* was scheduled to begin on Saturday, 27 April and all that morning we worked to coordinate the flights to and from the various Huaorani communities. Some of the delegates had to travel by foot or canoe to other communities in order to catch their flights, so the process had begun several days before. Supply planes had flown in to Toñampade in advance to drop off rice, meat, tinned fish, and other supplies, and the residents of Toñampade had built a large meeting space in the form of a traditional Huaorani A-frame house. I finally took a flight to Toñampade from Shell, arriving at 3:30 as the meeting was just getting underway. Delegates came from every single Huaorani community except Nemonpade, the community dominated by Stephen Saint. He had scheduled a large celebration and feast to coincide with the *Biye*, which all of the delegates and leaders whom I spoke with considered a direct attempt to sabotage the *Biye* and ONHAE. Saint's hostility toward ONHAE and the young generation of activists is well known. Mincaye Gilberto, a young man originally from Nemonpade (but who does not live there now) who was elected *conserje* at this *Biye* later told me that when Saint discovered that Mincaye would be attending the *Biye* and becoming active in the organization, Saint said: "ONHAE isn't good for anything. ONHAE isn't even an organization. ONHAE hurts the Huaorani people. ONHAE brings things that are horrible to the Huaorani. Christians know that ONHAE are communists.... I can provide everything that ONHAE can't."

The specially constructed meeting house for the event was an enormous traditional Huaorani house, approximately 25 by 50 feet (its ridgepole more than 20 feet off the ground), with ten rows of "benches" made from split tree trunks. A wooden desk had been brought in from the school, along with a chair, which was used by the meeting chairperson. There were about sixty delegates present when I arrived, including some ten women. The delegates represented a mix of ages, with many of the "*ancianos*" or older Huaorani (men and women) present; in fact, the delegates were generally older than the Huaorani population average (which is very young). This is interesting in light of the criticisms leveled at ONHAE by Stephen Saint and other evangelicals that ONHAE has excluded the older Huaorani from participation. The ratio of men to women was approximately 5:1, with about fifty men and ten women delegates present and in attendance on the first day. The chair presiding over the meeting on the first day was Mengotohue, the shaman from Quehueire Ono, who sat behind the desk and recognized individuals who wished to speak. Also seated at the front of the meeting were Boya and Rocio, who kept notes of all of the proceedings.[2] Boya was bare-chested and wore a traditional feather crown. Moi sat on one of the facing benches, in the front. By the end of the day, the number of delegates in attendance had grown to almost 100. In addition, students from the school (Toñampade has the only high school in Huaorani territory) were crowded around the outside entranceway of the hut listening to the proceedings. When recognized by the chair, speakers would stand at their seats and speak, sitting again when they had finished. There were no formal time limits once a speaker was recognized, and

The Biye. This outsized traditional Huaorani house was specially built for the meetings in Toñampade.

A woman addresses the Biye.

some spoke for a very long time. There was applause following every speaker, and more intense applause when someone said something very popular, but applause was also used throughout the *Biye* as a way to silence a speaker who had gone on too long. On this first day there also did not appear to be any agenda or specific subject matter to be discussed, but it soon became clear that they were in the process of establishing an agenda, albeit a somewhat loose one. The final agenda that emerged from the discussions on that first day was (1) land and border marking projects, (2) education, (3) health issues, and (4) tourism. The subject of new leadership was discussed, and was explicitly left until the end to decide.

When I arrived Boya introduced me to the assembly and asked me to speak briefly, which I did. Then Nanto (former president of ONHAE and current resident of Toñampade) spoke for almost forty-five minutes on a variety of themes: the need to be better organized, his desire to stop the oil companies, and the need to continue marking the borders of Huaorani territory. Dayuma also spoke at length and passionately about the need for the organization to be more representative of what the people want. While people spoke, a group of women, sometimes assisted by Boya, passed out candy and glasses of the sweet Kool Aid-type drink called Yupi. After a variety of other speakers had had a turn, the meeting broke up at a little before five P.M.

Dinner was served in one of the school buildings, with rice, tuna, and more Yupi. I chose to sit with some of the delegates I did not know (from the Cononaco and Yasuní groups); who told me that they knew the leadership was going to be replaced at this meeting but did not say that it would be by Moi. One person told me authoritatively that Moi was going to run against Nanto. After dinner I spoke with Moi, who told me that he would not face any opposition and that Boya was going to resign; he further said that he had been told this by Boya and that he and Boya were still friends.

The rest of the day the delegates socialized and played a ferocious game of soccer. Moi disappeared early and Boya went back to his family's compound of houses, which is located a short distance from the center of Toñampade with its airstrip, school, and missionary headquarters. I returned to Nancy's where I spoke at length with Dayuma and Nancy. Dayuma took me to see Rachel Saint's house and gravesite and spoke about the importance of ONHAE and the need for it to be more connected to the communities.

In the morning as I began to sit down to breakfast with Nancy, her son, and Dayuma, a boy arrived to ask me to accompany him to the house of Boya. I went with him and had breakfast with Boya (rice and tuna). Boya told me that he was not going to be replaced, but that all of the other elected officials were. He also told me that Moi would not have any position in the organization and that he had discussed all of this with Moi and that Moi had agreed. While I was at breakfast with Boya, I noticed that his family was in the process of constructing a new house in the compound. Boya told me that he didn't know who it was for. Later, one of his nephews told me that it was for Armando Boya.

From Boya's I went to the meeting house, where we had been told to gather at 8:00 A.M. By 8:30 it seemed that only about half the delegates were present. It soon became clear that many of the delegates had gone to church services. This seemed to enrage Boya, who stormed off yelling that the "evangélicos" had no right to interfere with ONHAE. Meanwhile, Moi took advantage of the moment and got himself in front of the forty or so delegates who were present to talk about rejecting the missionaries completely and being "real Huaorani again." He criticized the damage being done by outsiders, naming the missionaries and the oil companies. He spoke loudly and emotionally, yelling much of the time. While he spoke Boya returned and sat down briefly, but after less than a minute he got up and left.

Moi finished speaking at a few minutes past nine, as the rest of the delegates began filtering in, and Enquere checked them in with a roll call of each of the delegates' names. Nancy and Dayuma were among the last to arrive from the church services. When I asked what had taken place in the church I was able to elicit only vague responses.

By 10:00 A.M. the meeting was full, and an older woman spoke for a long time, criticizing Boya for his relationship with outsiders. When she had finished, Boya stood up and responded with a highly emotional, screaming speech. His voice cracked as he defended his actions and denied that he was friendly with the oil companies. Others, including Enquere, spoke at this point, but no one was paying any attention to them as both Boya and Moi had begun distributing gifts of combs and candy to the delegates. As a variety of people spoke about relations with outsiders it became clear that the subject was closely linked with ideas about money, and who (or what communities) would receive the goods and "*proyectos*" that the outsiders would bring. There were many complaints that the outsiders were only benefiting certain communities, while others received nothing.

For the rest of the afternoon the meeting followed a more or less regular agenda. The discussion focused on the project to demarcate the boundaries of Huaorani land. What was most interesting was that Moi and Boya sat next to each other for the entire afternoon, and Moi appeared to be dominating the meeting, getting up and speaking after each "rank-and-file" speaker finished. Boya said little that afternoon. The delegates remained seated in the meeting for most of the afternoon, while a group of women circulated with buckets of warm Yupi and paper cups. At the end of the afternoon the subject seemed to shift to the behavior and particularly the spending of the ONHAE leaders, and there was a discussion of whether the organization could survive without the financial support of the oil companies. Many of the delegates spoke about moving the ONHAE office to Toñampade so that the leadership would be in the forest, away from the undue influence of the companies and their wealth. Several speakers referred to the leaders becoming "confused" when they left the forest.

During this time Moi kept ostentatiously calling me up to the front of the meeting to ask me one or another question, most of them trivial. Finally I had to move to the front of the meeting myself because staying there would attract less attention than constantly making my way up through the crowd. Over lunch I had sat with Dayuma and Nancy and some of the delegates from Quenehuene. Their consensus evaluation of the meetings so far was that the office was definitely going to be moved and that the ONHAE leadership would spend most of its time in Toñampade. After lunch Moi disappeared from the meeting for about an hour, returning at 3:00 P.M. wearing a crown of feathers and carrying a long spear.

The Sunday afternoon session was dominated by some of the *ancianos* and women, who discussed education. Everyone called for the creation and maintenance of bilingual (Huao Terero/Spanish) schools. José Nango,[3] the director of education in the Huaorani schools, began to speak about education and was quickly challenged by Moi, who denied that he had the right to speak and further stated that the *Biye* should never be addressed in Spanish. Boya stepped in and took the part of José Nango, claiming that he could speak as an outsider. Boya and Moi then began to argue for the first time at the meeting, with Moi making a point-by-point refutation of each thing said by Boya. In the end Nango was given the opportunity to speak.

The meeting ended before dark, and after dinner most of the delegates were out in the fields playing soccer and socializing. I went to dinner with Boya at the house of José Nango. We talked about how the meetings were going, and Boya referred to his time as president (his "*etapa*") being over. Boya did not seem to be particularly busy, or worried about the outcome, but he did seem sad, and he avoided contact with the delegates and other leaders, returning by a roundabout route to his house and thus avoiding the soccer field area where most of the delegates were gathered.

Sunday night Moi came looking for me and asked me to translate a letter he had received from an agency of the United Nations looking into issues related to indigenous rights. The letter, which was in English, was an invitation for Moi to come and make a presentation to the investigating committee in Switzerland. I translated the letter into Spanish and explained as well as I could what it was about and what the United Nations was.

On Monday the discussion of education continued. This subject involved a number of contentious issues. There was debate over how many high schools there should be in Huaorani territory[4] and over whether, if there were to be only one high school, there should also be a "radio school" for students in other parts of the territory. An interesting component of the discussion was the constant reference to Maxus and Oryx as a source of funding for the schools. Despite the hostility that many of the delegates had shown toward the oil companies, as soon as the discussion turned to projects they wished to see carried out, the first source of funding that they mentioned was always the money supplied by the oil companies. Later in the morning many of the delegates, particularly the older ones, began criticizing the oil companies' actions in Huaorani territory, the existing *convenio*, and the relationship between the leadership of ONHAE and the companies. Boya responded angrily, shouting down some of the delegates and looking very uncomfortable. He made the statement that he was "disposed to cancel" the *convenio* and call for a moratorium, and that he did not want a new contract or *convenio* with Oryx. Other criticisms were leveled at the leaders at this time, most of which were based on the claim that they did not visit the communities often enough to know what the people wanted and what the problems were. After an hour and a half of this grilling, Boya left the front of the meeting and paced rapidly at the back, appearing very angry.

Monday afternoon the meeting moved on to the discussion of health issues. Nancy, as vice president for health, gave a long report after which there were some questions but not a great deal of acrimonious discussion as before. Even in the discussion of health issues, much of the focus was on what the oil companies should be paying and dissatisfaction with the way that the *convenio* had been implemented. Some of this focus was due to Moi's more or less constant commentary on the oil companies; he linked the oil companies (not without justification) to every single set of problems mentioned that day.

Finally, very late on Monday afternoon, the delegates began their discussion of tourism. Nanto spoke for a long time, issuing a rambling and angry denunciation of the way in which the tour guides profit from bringing people in to Huaorani territory without giving anything back to the communities that they visit. Then Moi spoke for a long time, and very enthusiastically, about "ecotourism" and about community-based tourist projects such as have been undertaken at Quehueire Ono. After he had spoken for about fifteen minutes, the delegates, appearing bored, clapped him down. Moi got up to speak again, this time reading aloud the letter from the UN that I had translated for him. He was using the letter to underscore the importance and fame of the Huaorani people throughout the world. By now the delegates were plainly tired of Moi, and while he continued to speak they were joking and laughing and getting up to go outside and take walks, although most of the delegates stayed around the meeting area. This was the first time the delegates had been disrespectful of any of the speakers at the meeting, a few going as far as to heckle Moi with calls of "*el loco*" and "*callate*" ("the crazy one" and "shut up").

Moi addresses the Biye.

The meeting broke up just before dusk, and the delegates played soccer and ate and joked. An interesting insight into the younger generations' view of traditional Huaorani practices came when Nanto and a group of about twenty young people began joking and telling stories near the soccer field. Nanto began joking about the old Huaorani customs, and then dropped his pants and put a string around his waist and tightly over his foreskin, laughing hilariously and saying that "I'm a Huao man" and "I'm a Tagaeri." This was greeted by howls of laughter from the others who were gathered around him.

At the same time Moi, Enquere, and a few other men were gathered in a classroom building discussing who should be in Moi's "cabinet" and what proposals he should put forward. They asked for my input and I said I didn't think it was certain yet what was going to happen the next day. Moi told me again that Boya was going to resign and that he (Moi) would run unopposed. I left Moi's meeting and found Toca, who told me that it was not certain that any of the leaders would be replaced. For all of the politicking that had gone on in the months leading up to the event, no one seemed to have a clear expectation of what would happen, or even a clear picture of the mood of the delegates.

On Tuesday morning as the meeting got underway after breakfast, Nanto brought in a blackboard from one of the classrooms. Boya was not yet present, and Mengotohue was not there either. The meeting was being chaired by Juan Huamoni, a very young man (who became president of ONHAE in 1998 and was subsequently jailed on suspicion of murder, probably a politically motivated charge). Juan spoke at length about the role of the *Biye* and its function as the supreme authority governing all of the actions of ONHAE, and he read selected passages from the ONHAE by-laws. While Juan Huamoni was still speaking he was interrupted by Moi, who spoke for a long time about how leaders should behave. Specifically, Moi said that the leadership should provide a careful accounting to the people of all money received and spent in a report every three months.

Following Moi, a number of delegates spoke about the idea of changing leaders at this meeting. Then Juan Huamoni took over again and read the requirements for an elected leader of ONHAE, which are:

1. Both parents must be Huaorani.
2. The candidate must speak "correct" Huao Terero.
3. The candidate must have lived the last four years in Huaorani territory.
4. The candidate may not belong to any other indigenous group.

While this discussion was going on Boya arrived. He was dressed in a variety of traditional and pseudo-traditional Huaorani regalia. His face was painted with *achiote*, and besides his gym shorts he wore only a chest piece made of woven leaves, arm bracelets, and an unusually elaborate and colorful feather crown. He carried a long wooden hunting spear and a traditional string bag.

As Boya was arriving, Rocio was placing a list of officers to be chosen on the blackboard. The list included president and vice presidents for "educación, tierra," and "salud" (education, land, and health). Boya began a long speech to the assembled delegates, who listened closely to him throughout, although he spoke for more than an hour and a half. He began to talk about gringos and about Quichuas (mentioning Delfin Andy by name). He screamed much of his speech, yelling that "we are not gringos, we are not Peruvians, we are Huaorani and Ecuadorians." He began to talk about allegations of corruption, and denied that he had ever done anything wrong as president. He bragged that he had gotten more money from the oil companies than any other president and that he had tried to administer the funds for projects to help improve the life of the people. As he spoke, he was interrupted twice by loud and raucous applause.

When Boya had finished a number of delegates, including Moi, spoke, each claiming that when leaders do wrong they must be replaced. Nanto rose and said that if the *Biye* wanted to replace some of the vice presidents because they weren't producing that was fine, but that the elected president should still serve out his full term as dictated in the by-laws of the organization. Enquere spoke next, saying that a president can't be replaced just because of suspicion; if someone is going to be accused of wrongdoing there must be proof, "like a canceled check or a receipt, otherwise it's just gossip."

Boya prepares to plead to the Biye that he be allowed to remain in office.

Moi got up next and began speaking, but none of the delegates paid much attention to him; many conversations began among the delegates at this time. Moi continued to speak (for more than an hour) despite the obvious lack of interest in what he was saying. He said that in order to run an organization like ONHAE one must have experience and that he, as one of the founders of the organization, had the necessary experience. He went on to say that on the one hand he was happy because the organization was now so much stronger than it had been at the beginning, but that on the other hand he was unhappy because it could be so much stronger and he could make it stronger.

At this point the order of the meeting itself began to break down. Nancy began to try to speak, but was cut off by Juan Huamoni. Moi began speaking again without having been recognized by the chair and was largely ignored by everyone. There were catcalls and someone (I could not identify who it was) shouted "Moi

Vicente, *el loco!*" José Nango began to speak (in Spanish) at the same time, urging the delegates not to change leaders without a compelling reason and stressing repeatedly (and inexplicably) that Boya was not really a drunk. Then Nanto translated what José had said into Huao Terero.

As Juan Huamoni began to get the meeting back under some kind of control, a number of delegates rose to speak, each of them saying that the president was all right, but that the vice presidents were not producing or doing their jobs well. Juan Huamoni then began to call on the delegates, one community at a time, asking whether the leaders should be replaced. Most of the delegates (including the delegates from Quehueire Ono) said that the president should not be replaced, but that the vice presidents should be removed. After this procedure, Juan Huamoni announced as chair that Boya would stay on as president, but new vice presidents would be selected.

Just as the decision to replace the vice presidents was announced, a plane began circling Toñampade's airfield, finally landing and coming to rest quite near the meeting house. Two North American missionaries got out, and much of the interest of the delegates was directed toward them. At this point they entered the *Biye* hut and sat down with the delegates.

Nanto rose and began to handle the nominations and elections, although Juan Huamoni continued to act as general meeting chair. Where seats were contested, Nanto put the names of the candidates on the board and conducted a roll call by community. A general vice president was chosen. New vice presidents were chosen for health, land, and tourism, and a new *conserje* was also chosen. Two of the vice presidential slots were contested; the others were selected by acclamation. None of the incumbent vice presidents (Toca, Nancy) entered the race or participated in the discussion at all.

Following the vote, Boya spoke again, much more calmly. He promised to seek other sources of funds beyond the oil company money and said that he did not want the Huaorani people to be dependent on the resources of the oil companies. Although his earlier speech had been given completely in Huao Terero, this time he spoke in a mix of Huao and Spanish. When he finished a num-

The results of the leadership elections. Hand votes were counted and recorded in front of the entire meeting.

ber of delegates asked questions, and several delegates asked him to move the office of ONHAE to Toñampade.

After Boya, Moi gave a passionate speech. He urged the organization to reject the oil companies completely, not to let them in to Huaorani territory and not to renegotiate any sort of *convenio* or contract. He spoke of the damage that oil exploration would do to the forest, and of the effects that the loss of the forest environment and the depletion of wildlife would have on the Huaorani people.

After Moi had finished there was a brief break for Yupi, and then a missionary named Dan (one of the two who had arrived in the plane) was introduced to the *Biye.* Dan spoke (in Spanish) to deny that the missionaries were discriminating against the bilingual schools, although he indicated that the missionaries did not like the schools. He also defended the decision to cut off support for a Huao school that had permitted its students to dance in the school building. This, he said, had violated the conditions set forth by the missionaries for financial support for education, so the school was closed.

During the lunch break Moi organized a group of people to go and tell a group of Quichua colonists somewhere nearby that they were in Huaorani territory. He suggested that there "may be some violence" and asked me to come with him. I declined; when I saw him again (in Puyo some weeks later) he said that nothing had come of it. It seemed perfectly clear to me at the time that Moi was uncomfortable and embarrassed after losing the election and being ridiculed, and that he was simply looking for a graceful way to leave the meetings.

The next morning the delegates lingered an unusually long time over breakfast, and everything indicated that they were becoming bored with the whole process. Attendance was down; people were coming to the meetings late and leaving frequently. There were many more side conversations going on than at the beginning of the *Biye* or during the "high drama" of the election of officers the day before. There were complaints about the food, and about the sleeping arrangements. Finally Boya and Toca went over to the building that was serving as the cafeteria and began shouting at the delegates to "be responsible" and come over to the meeting house so that they could get started. The meeting scheduled to begin at 8:00 A.M. finally got underway at a little after 9:15.

Juan Huamoni, who was chairing the meeting again, began by explaining that the only thing left to do was to approve a series of resolutions based on the discussions the delegates had been having all week. The proposed resolutions, prepared by Rocio and Boya, had been written out in Spanish. Juan Huamoni took a great deal of time to translate each one into Huao Terero. The resolutions covered each of the topics that had formed the agenda in the early days of the *Biye*. First, that the office of ONHAE was to be moved from Puyo to Toñampade, and that all of the officers were to begin to spend most of their time there. Second, to proceed with the border marking project to delineate the limits of Huaorani territory (*linderación*). Third, that all communities rejected in principle the idea of radio schools (*colegios de distancia*). Fourth, that Maxus would continue to provide aid for education and health to the communities. Fifth, that Maxus would provide outboard motors to each of the communities and a car for the use of ONHAE. Sixth, that the organization would begin to provide training in each of the communities for ecotourism projects. And finally, that absolutely no new agreements were to be signed by ONHAE leaders with any additional oil companies wishing to operate within Huaorani territory.

After the reading of the proposals there was a great deal of discussion, much of it very chaotic—Juan Huamoni seemed to lose control of the meeting at this point. Although voting (with a simple majority being decisive) is used to select candidates for office, policy resolutions require consensus. Everyone at the *Biye* must agree not to argue against the resolution in order for it to be approved. Although discussion in this case did not go on for more than a few hours, I was told by many current and former ONHAE leaders that discussion could continue until this elusive consensus was reached. Finally the resolutions were passed, in somewhat changed forms, and the business of the *Biye* was officially over. By this time the boredom of the delegates was palpable; although there had been more than one hundred delegates participating in the proceedings on the first and second days of the assembly, on this last day there were never more than seventy present at any one time, and many of those were not really paying attention to the proceedings. By this time too, the disquiet of the delegates was made worse by the constant rain. It had now rained more or less continuously for three days, and everyone was aware that no flights could come in or out of Toñampade until the airstrip had had a chance to dry out.

At the end of the *Biye* Nanto spoke for a long time about the need for the Huaorani to reject all outsiders, particularly all oil companies. He ridiculed Boya and his administration, and attacked Moi for forgetting about the Huaorani when he was with his new friends. The irony of Nanto saying this was not lost on the delegates, many of whom were discussing Nanto's speech after the meetings ended and all of whom (that I spoke with) pointed out that it was Nanto who had signed the first contract with an oil company to operate in Huaorani territory. The rest of the last day's meeting was given over to the teachers from the Huaorani high school in Toñampade, each of whom took turns thanking the delegates and talking about what each grade level in the school was doing. Most of the delegates paid little attention to this, and even while the meeting was still going on a soccer game began just outside of the meeting house.

That afternoon those delegates who could return to their communities by foot or canoe packed their things and left. The remainder, including myself, had to stay in Toñampade until the runway was safe to use again, which did not happen until Friday afternoon. After the flight back all of the (old) leaders met in the ONHAE office to discuss the *Biye* and then closed the office until Monday. Before we left, Boya called Milton Ortega at Maxus' community relations office and set up an appointment for Monday morning in the ONHAE office in Shell.

On Monday we were all in the office; I was typing the *Biye* resolutions, as approved, into the computer. Milton Ortega arrived at about 10:00 A.M. and after briefly greeting everyone, went into the large group meeting room with Boya. They made a point of closing the doors and windows (which quickly makes the room stuffy) and also closed the doors to the kitchen, where it might have been possible for someone to overhear their conversation.

When they had finished meeting, Boya and Milton Ortega came into the office where I was working and had me make changes in the resolutions that had been passed by the *Biye*. The changes were relatively minor, but they were designed to remove responsibility from Maxus. For example, the resolution that stated that the *Biye* would demand that Maxus should provide outboard motors and an automobile for ONHAE was changed to say that ONHAE would "seek financing" for such activities. The changes may have been minor, but it was clear that Boya had been working with Milton Ortega on the resolutions themselves, and that they had agreed on certain changes to be made in the actual wording of the documents approved by the full *Biye*.

Observations

As was stated in the introduction to this chapter, I believe that the *Biye* provides us with the opportunity to observe many of the organizational and interpersonal dynamics that shape the behavior and efficacy of ONHAE. Many of my conclusions, particularly where they delve into questions of motivation for actions, are necessarily speculative; nevertheless, I believe that one may draw some inferences about internal ONHAE politics, relationships, and possible

stresses from the behavior of the parties to the disputes at and surrounding the *Biye*. The *Biye* is, according to the by-laws of the organization, the supreme authority of ONHAE. It is charged with
setting the policies for the organization as well as selecting its leaders. Apart from the still unstandardized process of the selection and
apportionment of the delegates from the communities, as a decision making body its internal workings are as "democratic" as it is
possible to be. All of the decisions of the *Biye* are founded on consensus rather than a simple majority rule. The process of deter-
mining the resolutions of the meeting is most similar to a Quaker
meeting for business: there is a discussion period, following which
some designated person or persons are asked to put into words the
"sense of the meeting." If no one objects to this statement of consensus, it will become the meeting's resolution of the question. It
also builds on traditional Huaorani practices, and ONHAE's
founders and leaders have worked to create the sense that in some
way the modern *Biye* represents an extension of traditional forms of
intergroup dialogue and dispute resolution, although this archaism
seems extremely idealistic.

The leadership of ONHAE has developed its own style of politics, as well as its own rifts, disputes, and competing interest
groups. Within the leadership cadre itself,[5] disputes such as that
between Moi and Boya are rarely spoken of directly. The dispute is
masked by apparent friendliness and comradeship, while each
works intently to prevail over the other. In the case of this dispute,
it was clear that Moi wanted several things: he wanted the prestige
and power that went with the title and office of president, he
wanted to change the policies of ONHAE so as to remove the oil
companies from Huaorani territory, and he wanted to thus secure
his position among the environmentalists and intellectuals who
looked to him already as the de facto "representative" of the Huaorani. Boya also wanted the power and prestige associated with the
office, but more than that, Moi's challenge represented a challenge
to his reputation as a Huaorani man and as a leader; to be replaced
in the middle of his term would have been a humiliating defeat for
him and he had no choice but to fight to maintain his position.
Another aspect of the Moi/Boya conflict was the extent to which
their relative support was misjudged by both principals and their

supporters (both Huaorani and *cowode*). Boya truly believed that Moi represented a threat to him, and he campaigned accordingly. Moi also misjudged his own strength, which showed itself at the *Biye* to be minimal or nonexistent. In fact, one of the things that I found to be truly remarkable at the *Biye* was the way in which I too had misjudged Moi's popularity and influence among the Huaorani. For westerners, Moi's clear, consistent, and vocal interest in preserving the forest is appealing in a way that no other Huaorani leader can emulate. Moi presents himself as a leader of the Huaorani, and is certainly one of the least self-effacing of the Huaorani leadership. In his own community of Quehueire Ono he has been a leader, and has been instrumental in the establishment of an ongoing ecotourism project and other undertakings. However, his concern with relatively abstract questions of environmental preservation has failed to connect him with the majority of the Huaorani people. When he spoke at the *Biye* it quickly became clear that he had no real support among the delegates, and that they saw him as somewhat crazy and undependable. However, the niche that he has very effectively carved out for himself within the organization, as the de facto Huaorani ambassador to the national and global environmental and human rights movements, remains crucial.

The relationship between the organizational leadership and the various interested outside agents operating around the Huaorani is also highlighted by the case of the *Biye*. The Huaorani remain outside of the capitalist relations of production that have come to dominate the so-called "global economy." They view their own leaders as well as all outsiders as potential sources of resources, resources that may be "gathered" like any other. Throughout the *Biye* a consistent refrain was "look what I have brought you." This success at bringing goods and other resources into the communities from the *cowode* was used as a justification for leaders continuing in office, and many of the delegates' complaints were focused on the idea that ONHAE should have been able to get more. Clearly this emphasis on "outsiders" as a source of goods represents a fundamental impediment to the ideas of conservation, preservation of the forest, and rejection of oil exploitation.

The oil companies were not the only group treated in this way in the discourse of the *Biye*. Environmentalists and ecotourists were also seen as sources of goods and income. Boya bragged on a number of occasions that the Rainforest Action Network had financed the *Biye*, and the missionary groups were also viewed as welcome contributors. However, the Huaorani relationship with North American missionaries is clearly a more complex and problematic one, complicated, I believe, by the emphasis in the missionaries' discourse on their desire to "help" the Huaorani, and by their long history of very paternalistic contact. Many of the Huaorani leaders seemed to be afraid to publicly criticize the activities of the missionaries, as was evidenced by Boya's silence at the *Biye*, despite his privately expressed anger, about the many delegates who had skipped the Sunday morning meetings to attend church services, and by the willingness of all of the delegates to permit the North American missionary Dan to formally address the meeting. Despite his involvement in the closing of a school that had permitted dancing, there was notably little criticism leveled at him or the missionary school administration. In fact, he was greeted effusively by many of the delegates, who clustered around him, hugging and touching him. But later, once Dan had departed, many of these same delegates bitterly criticized the actions of the missionaries and of the missionary school administration in particular.

Finally, the *Biye* represents an important case study in evaluating the ability of a previously "acephalous" or leaderless group to begin to adapt forms of centralized "self-government" to their culture and society. First, it is noteworthy that the *Biye*, although in truth an entirely new form for the Huaorani, has been invested with an artificial tradition and "time-depth" by invoking the idea of an intergroup conference that ostensibly took place in the past. This fits Patterson's (1993: 338) definition of archaism—"the imitation of something old and its incorporation into new contexts." Second, the forms adopted as the structure of the *Biye*, although they borrow heavily from existing Quichua and Shuar organizational forms, avoid the obvious imposition of the will of one group on another; by seeking consensus in the approval of policy resolutions the *Biye* avoids creating "losers" in the policy debates. All of this is indicative of a sort of democratic decision making process; however, the subsequent "tinkering" with the resolutions after the dissolution of the formally constituted *Biye*, coupled with the involvement of the oil companies, points to a process that is flawed in its execution by the leadership's lack of accountability to those who made up the *Biye* that set the policy. For a number of reasons, the great majority of the delegates to the *Biye* are unable to effectively verify anything about the fealty of the ONHAE leadership/administration to the principles and policies laid out by the assembly: first, because the majority of the delegates come from fairly isolated communities that have little communication with the leadership other than during an assembly; second, because in dealings with the *cowode* many of the delegates lack the sophistication to effectively evaluate the nuances of changes in the implementation of *Biye* policy; and finally, because the chief source of information about how the leadership is implementing the decisions of the *Biye* is the leadership itself.

Thus accountability becomes a problematic issue for ONHAE and other similarly situated indigenous organizations. The decisions of the *Biye* are not universally respected as they should be according to the organization's own charter, and the leadership largely operates in a vacuum far apart from the majority of Huaorani. The leaders also live apart from the Huao population, leaving them open to the blandishments and sophisticated pressures that can be mustered in defense of the interests of multinational oil companies or North American evangelical Christian missionaries.

Part Two: La Feria del Puyo

Another useful case study is presented by the activities of ONHAE in organizing Huaorani participation in the annual "Feria del Puyo" (Puyo town fair) parade. ONHAE's activities in this instance can shed light on the relationship between the Huaorani people and the mestizo and other indigenous populations of the Ecuadorian *oriente*, and on the representations and mythology surrounding the Huaorani in local and regional contexts. The ONHAE-sponsored Huaorani presence in the parade, the representations of Huaorani culture, history, and traditions in the parade, and the dress and behavior of the ONHAE leadership each present the observer with useful illustrations of Huaorani perceptions of themselves and of their understanding of the myths surrounding their culture. The ethnic entrepreneurs who serve as the leadership of ONHAE are aware of the stereotypes of the Huaorani in the national discourse, and use selected elements of these stereotypes to gain access to the mestizo-dominated world outside of Huaorani territory.

The Feria del Puyo is an annual event that includes dances, competitive events (cockfights and soccer games), an amusement park set up in the town square with rides and games, and a large parade that marks the culmination of the fair. It is a celebration of the founding of the city, supposedly on the twelfth of May. At one time the event was celebrated on a single day, but it is now a four-day extravaganza, drawing visitors from all parts of the *oriente* and even from Quito and other highland cities. Throughout the fair there is a great deal of drinking, with many fairgoers drinking until they lose consciousness.

Planning and preparation for the parade in 1996 began months before, when schools, fraternal organizations, military and veteran's organizations, businesses, and indigenous organizations were invited to participate in the parade. ONHAE received a letter from the *alcalde* (mayor) of Puyo, asking them to participate for the first time. Initially the letter suggested that participants should represent the Huaorani high school in Toñampade, but soon the leadership of ONHAE had begun to plan a much more ambitious presence in the event. Boya and Toca contacted Milton Ortega of Maxus and, reminding him that he had not had to pay for the *Biye*, asked him to pay for the flights of Huaorani students, teachers, and others from Toñampade and other communities to Puyo for the parade. Ortega agreed to pay for a limited number of flights. Then Boya solicited free flights from Alas de Socorro, the missionary flight service that is intimately connected with all of the schools in Huaorani territory. They agreed to supply several additional flights.

Once this was accomplished, Boya himself went to Toñampade to work with the school personnel on the plans for the parade. A few days before the parade was scheduled to take place, several of the teachers from Toñampade came to Shell and worked to put together some of the floats. They also had the use of a truck belonging to the Ecuadorian Ministry of Education.

On the day of the parade, more than one hundred Huaorani children and adults, as well as virtually all of the mestizo and

Quichua school personnel, were flown out of Toñampade, Quehueire Ono, and other communities to participate. In Puyo, virtually the entire town turned out to watch the parade. The streets
were lined with spectators, vendors, and police (extra police were
brought in from other cities during the fair). The parade began by
marching through the central plaza and then wound its way
through most of the major streets of the city. The mayor and a
group of local dignitaries (mostly business leaders), dressed in business suits, marched at the head of the line. Among the dignitaries
were representatives of indigenous organizations, including Boya,
Toca, and Mengotohue from ONHAE. They were followed by a
military honor guard, and then by the entire army brigade head-
quartered at the Shell base, and the local militia. This display of
Ecuadorian military might was notable for its lack of order and the
poor condition of their uniforms and frequently outdated weapons
(M-14s and .30-caliber semiautomatic carbines).

Local officials and dignitaries kick off the Feria del Puyo.

Feria del Puyo. An honor guard from the base in Shell.

This was followed by a succession of neighborhood, community, and social organizations, each representing a particular barrio or association of barrios, with banners identifying them. OPIP and the Federación Shuar each had fairly small contingents in this part of the parade. Several fraternal organizations came next, and then an interminable succession of floats representing each grade of each school in the province. Each of these had a musical theme, usually a current salsa or meringue hit song (*El Venado* was inexplicably popular with younger groups), and the students, in costume, danced in unison (more or less) to the music. Each group followed a pickup truck or automobile equipped to blare the music at the highest possible volume. City and provincial workers, churches, and several private businesses also had floats or displays in the parade.

The Huaorani segment of the parade was one of the largest individual parts. More than sixty Huaorani took part, as well as at least twelve non-Huaorani school employees. As will be discussed below, all of the Huaorani participants who had been brought in for the parade were dressed in ersatz "traditional" clothing. The Huaorani parade contingent included five discrete segments: "Ahumado del Pescado" (smoking fish); "Elaboración de la Chicha" (making *tepe*); "Guerra Tradicional Huaorani" (traditional Huaorani warfare); "Matrimonio Huaorani" (Huaorani marriage); and "Juventud Huaorani" (Huaorani youth).

At the front of the Huaorani contingent a group of four well-dressed schoolteachers carried a banner that read "Huaponi Huaorani" on the first (top) line and "Amigos Huaoranis" on the second line. A list of the schools in Huaorani territory followed. *Huaponi* (more often spelled *waaponi*) is a Huao word that means variously hello, goodbye, thanks, and good.

The first two segments of the Huaorani/ONHAE contingent included floats assembled on trailers pulled by a Ministry of Education van. On the first float a group of Huaorani women were tending a real fire in a packed earthen hearth, over which hung a number of extremely large river catfish. Other women on the float were cutting up smoked fish in tiny portions and placing them on paper plates, while another group of women picked up the plates of fish and passed them out to the crowd. At the side of the float was a mestiza woman schoolteacher dressed in a navy blue business suit and carrying a long-handled, hand-lettered sign that read "Ahumado del Pescado."

Immediately behind came the second float, on which a number of women of mixed ages were mixing fermented *yuca* paste with water to make Huaorani *tepe*. On this float a sort of "kitchen" had been set up, with grass and dirt spread on the floor of the trailer to simulate a jungle house interior. Another teacher, this time a man in a navy blue suit, carried a sign reading "Elaboración de la Chicha."[6] The *tepe* was served in tiny plastic cups, and young women were passing the cups to the spectators. Although many of the parade watchers received samples of the fish and *tepe*, many did not eat the fish, and almost no one drank the *tepe*. In a few cases individuals dared others to take a sip of the tepe, but most of it was just thrown out. There was much laughter over this, and some open signs of revulsion. Twice I heard different individuals warn that "you mustn't make them angry with you" because "they may become violent."

The third segment was composed of a group of Huaorani men carrying spears. Their faces were painted with designs of red *achiote* and some were wearing feathered crowns. For most of the parade the men chanted a traditional Huao song. Several times they acted

Feria del Puyo. "Elaboración de la chicha" (making tepe). Huaorani women in ersatz "traditional" dress mix tepe and distribute cups to the crowd.

out a sort of skit graphically depicting the spearing of an imaginary opponent. The sign accompanying this, carried by a schoolteacher again, proclaimed "Guerra Tradicional Huaorani."

Feria del Puyo. Their faces painted, Huaorani men carrying spears re-enact "traditional warfare."

Feria del Puyo. A miniature traditional Huaorani house is used as a float to illustrate "Matrimonio Huao" (Huaorani marriage).

The next section, identified by the sign "Matrimonio Huao," included a hand-carried replica in miniature of a traditional Huaorani house, which had been hastily built the night before. This float was accompanied by approximately twenty women, most carrying palm fronds. There were also several women carrying infants. No men were visible in this segment of the parade. It seems that marriage was being presented as something of interest to, and involving, women more than men.

The final Huaorani segment of the parade, "Juventud Huaorani," consisted of a group of young students from the Huaorani schools. Many of the smaller children looked frightened, and the teacher in charge of this section, who was carrying the sign, kept yelling at them to stay in line and not to bunch up around her.

All of the Huaorani participants had their faces painted with red *achiote* and were dressed in "outfits" devised by the missionaries to represent traditional Huaorani "clothing." These outfits are made of a woven bark cloth that is stretched around the waist of the wearer, resembling the sort of "micro-mini" that might have been worn by a 1960s cocktail waitress. Some women wrapped a second four-to six-inch-wide strip around their chest to cover their breasts, while other women simply wore brassieres. This "traditional" clothing is, of course, a complete invention. Before missionary contact, all Huaorani went without any clothing whatsoever except a string tied around the waist. Men wore it tight around their foreskin; women wore it a bit looser. In a number of downriver groups on the Cononaco and Yasuní rivers Huaorani still "dress" in this way. When the missionaries arrived, they forced the Huaorani to adopt western-style clothing, which they distributed to them. In most Huaorani communities today, it is unusual to see anyone without at least some sort of covering on their lower bodies, although bare-breasted women are not uncommon except in missionary centers, where they are only very rarely seen. At no time did the Huaorani ever engage in the manufacture of garments from forest materials. At the same time, many of the participants in the parade wore intricately woven feathered crowns and armbands, which did exist as a part of Huaorani material culture before missionary contact was established. The painting of faces, and in some cases of feet or arms, with *achiote* is also a tradition that is rooted within Huaorani history.

While the parade was in progress, the leaders of ONHAE circulated among the Huaorani parade participants, the dignitaries, and the crowd. Occasionally they participated in the parade itself, at which moments they were conspicuous by their dress and demeanor. The leaders who were present at the event included Boya, Toca, and Enquere. They wore clean western-style clothes. Boya, for example, wore jeans and a button front collar shirt with sneakers. None of the leaders painted their faces, carried spears or other "jungle" accoutrements, or wore feathers or any other sign that they were Huaorani. These three participated in the opening ceremonies at the start of the parade, where they appeared on the stage in the town square with the mayor of Puyo, other politicians, military officers, and other dignitaries.

Following the parade, as the town settled down to a large, raucous, and intermittently violent drinking party, the Huaorani parade participants gathered together in an open lot away from the festivities. At this time Boya put on a feathered crown, and Toca had his face painted with achiote. A number of the older Huaorani men spent some time chanting and singing, and then the Huaorani

Feria del Puyo. The current and past presidents of ONHAE accompany the parade in western-style clothing.

who had come in from the communities went back to Shell and stayed there until the next day, when they began the process of returning home. Boya and Toca returned to the festivities in Puyo, where they sat in a bar (drinking only soft drinks) and quietly watched the fiesta.

The Huaorani participation in the parade is illustrative in a number of ways. Viewed as a performance, it can be perceived as a sort of theater, in which the leadership of ONHAE played an intermediary role acting as the link between the Huaorani communities and the predominantly mestizo parade organizers. More significantly, the leadership also acted to design a performance in which the cultural stereotypes of the Huaorani were accentuated and placed in the foreground. The parade featured the Huaorani as (almost) naked, as killers, and as jungle dwellers living a "savage" life. The parade served to reinforce the prevailing stereotypes of the Huaorani as the national "savages" they have often been portrayed as in both Ecuadorian and international media (see Rival 1994: 253-88). The leaders themselves did not take direct part in this caricature of Huaorani life, but they used it as a way to strengthen their position in both societies. They provided Huaorani "color" for the parade in this intermediary role, but by their dress and demeanor they sought to separate themselves from the life of the Huaorani people in the communities, or at least from the national stereotypes of that life. The representation of Huaorani life depicted a synthetic, ahistorical, pre-contact past but was not identified as history–the implication of the event was that this is both a current and an accurate illustration of Huaorani life. I asked Boya about the depiction of the Huaorani in the parade, and he told me that "this was what they [the parade organizers] expected." In discussions with young Huaorani I found substantial pride in the reputation for ferocity and toughness enjoyed by the Huaorani. Gilberto, a young Huao who has since taken a role in the ONHAE leadership, commented that the Huaorani can get what they want from other indigenous groups and the mestizo-dominated state because "they are all afraid of us." Moi, as well, has learned to present himself and Huaorani culture as "exotic" and to emphasize a closeness with nature when speaking with ecotourists, while stressing the ferocity of the Huaorani when engaged in dialogue with Ecuadorians. Muratorio (1982) has described this phenomenon in the context of *mestizaje* and ethnic identity in highland Ecuador. It is in the interests of the ruling classes of the national state to homogenize the population and create a broader sense of "nationality" while extending the myth of mestizo sameness. Ethnicity is reduced to a caricature of "typical" dress, foods, and so on that Muratorio aptly calls an "alienated folkloric consciousness."

Whitten (1985: 217-45) analyzed the 12 May Puyo parade of 1981–before ONHAE, and before the regular and continuous presence of Huaorani in the city. He describes a similar role being played then by Quichua and Shuar parade participants. He argues that these representations of indigenous "savages" provide "contrast sets" against which to portray the civility and development of Puyo and the developmentalist nationalism of Ecuador. Ideological constructions at the heart of modern Ecuador, *mestizaje*, progress and development, can thus be projected against their opposite–the naked, childlike, violent savage of the forest. That may be the supportive ideological role ascribed to the Huaorani parade contingent, but for the leaders of ONHAE participation in the parade represents a way to enhance their position as ethnic entrepreneurs vis-á-vis the regional mestizo elites, and to gain access to and gratitude from those elites. This access and recognition serves to validate their own position as leaders, and thus to strengthen their position in dealings with other *cowode*, including oil and governmental representatives.

Notes

1. AEROPIP has only two planes, and the sole private charter service operating out of the Shell airport has only one (working) plane. Alas de Socorro has six planes capable of making the difficult landings on the short dirt and grass airstrips found in Huaorani communities.
2. As will be discussed, the proceedings were largely conducted in Huao Terero, which Rocio does not speak.
3. José Nango is a government employee who has worked with the Huaorani schools for many years. He is married to a Huaorani woman, and they live in Toñampade in their own private house, not in the provided teachers housing.
4. At the time of the 1996 *Biye*, the only schooling available beyond the fourth or fifth grade was in Toñampade, the location of the only Huaorani high school or "*colegio.*".
5. I have chosen to use the word *cadre* here to include that group of leaders/organizers clustered around ONHAE. This I understand to include current and former elected leaders, members of the founding group of ONHAE, and the "hangers on" and other participants who are most likely to hold leadership posts in the future.
6. "Chicha" is the Quichua word for a drink similar to what the Huaorani call *tepe*. The word chicha has been adopted in Spanish as well.

Chapter 4

TOWARD AN ORGANIZATIONAL EVALUATION

Perhaps inevitably, ONHAE was formed at a moment of crisis for the Huaorani people. Organizing of any sort takes place only when such urgency is present. The relative stability of the first post-contact decades was breaking down as some Huaorani began to reject the missionary control of their lives, and as the oil companies began to enter their territory in earnest. Previously the Huaorani had responded to perceived threats in one of three ways: violence, as in the famous cases of the killings of missionaries and oil company workers in 1956, 1973, and 1983; avoidance and retreat from the threat, as when the Huaorani were known to hide and flee to avoid the rubber tappers (or as in the famous case of the Tagaeri); or acquiescence and surrender, as occurred when the Huaorani allowed themselves to be missionized and placed on a reservation in the 1960s. ONHAE represents a new sort of response for the Huaorani, one copied from their indigenous neighbors. As has been pointed out by Siracusa (1996: 192-93) from the beginning of ONHAE's organizational history its work has been focused on the specific relations between it and the oil companies in their territory. This work has subsumed and overshadowed the leaders' efforts to

---

Notes for this section can be found on page 154.

legalize their territorial claims, and their relationships with other indigenous organizations and federations.

In order to begin to evaluate the effectiveness of an organization, its goals must be made explicit so that the degree to which such goals have been met can begin to be assessed. In the case of an ethnicity-based advocacy organization like ONHAE, there may be many "goals" (or perhaps "hopes") at the time of founding. Such aspirations are not fixed and usually change over time. For the Huaorani, there were a number of critically important, explicitly stated goals, as well as other, implicit, aspirations. Over time, as the organization succeeded in establishing itself as the representative of the Huaorani people, other ways of thinking about their role became part of the leaders' thought and rhetoric. The first part of this chapter will identify these concrete and explicitly stated goals of ONHAE, and evaluate the organization's efforts to meet them through the time of my fieldwork. There follows, in the second part, a discussion of the intangible goals and struggles of the organization and its leaders in their attempts to situate themselves as Huaorani within national, regional, and indigenous spheres as well as their process of definition of what it means to be "Huaorani" and how the culture, gender roles and other aspects of Huao society have been affected by the process of organizing.

Part One

ONHAE's explicitly stated goals include the legalization, delineation, and protection of territorial integrity; the protection of the forest from the depredations of the oil companies; and the facilitation of improvements in the systems of education and health care for all of the Huaorani people. The three vice-presidential positions, discussed earlier, are indicative of these priorities–one each for land, health, and education. All of these goals are intimately linked with the relationships existing between ONHAE and the oil companies. Obviously the land itself is under threat from the activities of the oil companies, but it is the oil companies that are being asked to finance any improvements in health care or education for the Huaorani people. I cannot judge the extent to which the strategies of ONHAE have been planned in advance, but I do know that by using the rhetoric of the environmental movement, and by stating periodically that they want the complete withdrawal of the oil companies from their territory, the Huaorani leaders have been able to extract from the companies more and more support for schools and health care. This strategy, however, fails to take into account several problems: first, the long-term damage and eventual destruction of the Huaorani traditional lands; second, the sheer paucity of the company's contributions in light of the value of the oil being taken out; and finally, the debilitating effect of Huaorani agreements on the negotiating positions of the other indigenous groups, who depend on interethnic solidarity to maintain their strength in confrontations with the oil companies and the state.

The expressed goals of ONHAE are similar to those of other indigenous organizations in the region, particularly in the emphasis on land rights. This paramount issue is the basis for the negotiations with oil interests, missionaries, and the state. For example, the *Federación de Organizaciones Indígenas del Napo* (Federation of Indigenous Organizations of Napo–FOIN), a Quichua organization in the neighboring province of Napo, states: " The primary objectives of the FOIN ... are: the defense of our permanently threatened territory and the defense of our culture" (CONAIE 1989: 48). MacDonald (1995a: 10), discussing ethnic federations in the Ecuadorian Amazon, states:

> Most federations maintain three primary concerns: 1) the defense of their member communities' rights to land and resources and; 2) the expansion and strengthening of their organizations; 3) the maintenance of their unique ethnic identity. In many ways they resemble other popular organizations; however, their insistence on maintaining their distinct cultural identity differentiates them from labor unions, peasant leagues and similar social sectors in Latin America.

Land figures so prominently in all of these organizing efforts because for the Huaorani, as for most of the indigenous peoples of the Amazon, land is the basis for the construction of the social organization of production. This is what Richard Lee (2000: 7) calls the "sense of place" of indigenous peoples. Certainly for the Huaorani, space is understood not in terms of ownership per se, in the western sense, but as a multi-layered system of rights and responsibilities–hunting, usufruct rights, residential rights, etc. (Rival 1998: 635-39) More than any other feature of indigenous organizing, the securing of land rights is indispensable if indigenous groups hope to maintain their distinct identities over time. As Lee (2000: 23) says, "On meaningful work there is no substitute for winning land rights as a way of conferring dignity and self-reliance." The Huaorani, although numbering less than two thousand persons, have succeeded in establishing legal title to an extremely large territory, although this territorial title does not give the Huaorani control over the subsurface mineral rights. As discussed in Chapter 2, this "victory" was achieved in large part because it provided the government with a way to permit the exploitation of oil reserves in areas that had previously been designated as a "biosphere preserve" subject to strict international control.

One of the primary responsibilities of the vice president for land issues is the ongoing process of *linderación* or border marking. This is probably the most ambitious project undertaken directly by the organization, involving crude surveying in some of the remotest parts of the Ecuadorian rainforest and tremendously hard work in planting a border of palm trees that serve to demarcate the boundaries of Huaorani territory. The primary reason mentioned for the replacement of Toca as the vice president for land was precisely that he had not organized a *jornada de linderación* during his tenure.

In the area of education, the organization has been instrumental in establishing schools throughout the territory, and in giving the Huaorani people relatively more control over the schools, and the missionaries relatively less. It is this new autochthonous control of the schools that I believe stands as the greatest accomplishment of ONHAE in the field of education. Previously, the schools that did exist were controlled exclusively by the North American evangelical missionaries. During the 1960s and early 1970s Rachel Saint was given control of the schools in the "Protectorate" by the Ecuadorian government–and the SIL established and ran a number of schools in those communities within this reservation. After the expulsion of the SIL (1973-74) they continued to function as missionary schools, while new schools, with teachers paid by the government, were established in the other communities. The communities where most Huaorani live today are typically centered around an airstrip and a school. The Huaorani see schools as a critical component in "civilizing" children and making them capable of interacting with the *cowode* world–a highly valued skill set (see Rival 1992: 216-19). As has been discussed by Rival (1992: 226-32 and 420-26) the schools' curriculum is still based on the national curriculum set by the Ministry of Education and includes the national and nationalist ideological constructions set by that agency. A key component of this curriculum is the ideology of *mestizaje,* which is found in the government-provided textbooks and coursework.[1]

In those schools that are still administered by the evangelicals strict rules are in place governing the curriculum, codes of student (and teacher) behavior, and religious education. These rules may vary somewhat from school to school because individual churches or missionary societies in the United States are sponsors of individual schools and are permitted to establish rules for those schools. As was mentioned in Chapter 3, one school lost its missionary funding after a teacher permitted the students in the school to dance.

The Huaorani desire to have control over education in the territory is reflected in this resolution passed by the 1995 *Biye*: "The aid to education in the Huaorani zone, (supplies, uniforms, food, money, flights, etc.) that comes from the Evangelical mission ... oil companies, or others must occur without any conditions, otherwise it will be rejected and investigated by ONHAE." In practice, however, it is extremely difficult for any Huaorani leader to reject offers of aid and assistance, even when they come with implicit or explicit conditions. This is particularly true given the tendency for Huaorani leaders to take credit (or blame) for the goods and/or *proyectos* they have been able to bring in to the communities.

One of the educational accomplishments (mentioned above) of ONHAE has been the establishment of bilingual (Spanish and Huao Terero) education in many of the village schools. Demanding bilingual education is seen as a way of preserving the Huaorani language and culture, and is something that has been copied from the experiences of the Quichua and Shuar organizations, which have made bilingual education a cornerstone of their education policies.

It is also through these organizations that bilingual education has come to be an official part of government educational policy for schools in indigenous communities. The Huaorani thus benefited from a many years-long struggle by their indigenous comrade organizations in which they themselves had not taken a meaningful part. The bilingual teachers are Huaorani, who work together with a mestizo or Quichua teacher; both are hired and paid by the government's Ministry of Education. In one community in the old SIL Protectorate, Tihueno, a bilingual education program was discontinued after being well established, and the residents express hostility to the idea of bilingual education. However, this seems to be the result of one extremely harsh Huaorani teacher who used corporal punishment on the students in his charge. The Huaorani do not hit children as a regular part of child-rearing discipline, and the parents in Tihueno were extremely upset when this occurred, leading to their demand that the teacher be removed.

There has also been a campaign of school building undertaken by ONHAE and carried out largely with funding from the oil companies. The buildings that have been constructed are solid and spacious, raised on pillars two to four feet off the ground, with tin roofs. They are, however, made of wood, which although treated will not last long under jungle conditions. Several Huaorani parents complained that the buildings were not cement, which would last much longer. The oil companies and ONHAE take credit for the buildings and show them off as great accomplishments resulting from their *acuerdo*. In Toñampade, for instance, many of the school buildings are painted with either the Petroecuador logo or with the words "*Convenio*: ONHAE-MAXUS 1994." In fact the cost of such buildings to Maxus is minimal, involving perhaps a few hundred dollars' worth of materials and a single helicopter flight into the community. It is indicative of the relatively light demands that ONHAE has so far made on the oil companies that such minor gifts represent the only tangible fulfillment of the company's promises.

In the area of health care, ONHAE has, as in education, taken over some of the administrative functions that were previously carried out by the missionaries. Once again, the most significant change that has taken place in this arena is the shifting of control over these services to the Huaorani themselves, as the organization.

Huaorani needing health care are no longer supplicants receiving the charity of the missionaries, but instead are demanding only that which has already been agreed to in the *convenio.* But once again, the health programs of ONHAE depend on financing obtained largely through the oil companies. Some missionary health care work does still take place (particularly vaccination programs), but although the missionary workers seek permission from ONHAE before beginning a project, they generally do not give ONHAE administrative control (or credit).

Although the *convenio* between ONHAE and Maxus calls on Maxus to pay for Huaorani health care, this has been a constant problem, as described in Chapter 2. In practice, Maxus has spent little in fulfillment of a contract that at best would represent no significant percentage of Maxus' profits from oil from Huaorani territory. Periodically this has resulted in a crisis when the missionary hospital in Shell (Hospital Vozandes del Oriente) has stopped accepting Huaorani patients without prepayment by ONHAE. Although the leadership of ONHAE has bitterly criticized this failure to live up to the agreement on the part of Maxus, they have no mechanism by which to compel compliance, as the agreement is not a legal contract.

Part Two

As successive administrations have pursued these goals they have also discovered new goals having to do with the unity of the Huaorani and with the image and role of the Huaorani people in the national and regional contexts. The very fact of being an organization whose base is defined by ethnicity makes the maintenance and definition of that ethnic identity a priority for the successful reproduction of the organization through time. Certainly the Huaorani leaders have had to define who is and who is not a Huaorani, and they spoke frequently of the uniqueness and value of Huaorani culture.

Incidental to the pursuit of the concrete goals discussed in Part One has been the development of a new ethnic consciousness–a new self-definition of what it means to be "Huaorani." Ethnicity is socially constructed in large measure through the definition and identification of nonmembers and boundaries (cultural and/or geographic). Traditional Huaorani society, which viewed only members of related *nanicabos* as Huaorani–and other speakers of Huao Terero as *Huarani* ("other people") has been replaced by a new pan-Huaorani consciousness. This part of ONHAE's experience grows, in part, out of the constant contact it has with a wide variety of non-Huaorani, most of whom claim to be the allies or "friends" of the Huaorani. The non-Huaorani participants in the indigenous movement, as well as the environmental, socialist, and progressive organizations, all claim their solidarity and commonality with the struggles of the Huaorani. The oil companies and the Protestant missionaries profess friendship and respect for the organization, but they also want the Huaorani organization to behave as these outside groups would prefer. Further, each of these groups actively attempts to limit the influence of some of the other outside groups.

One of the greatest and most misunderstood successes of ONHAE has been the maintenance of its institutional independence. Although ONHAE has continued to work with the environmental, indigenous-rights, and socialist groups that claim to be its allies, it has never become subservient to them. In terms of outcomes, this may not have been a good thing for the Huaorani people, and in many cases ONHAE may have settled for far less than it could have gotten had it maintained solidarity with these other groups. Clearly the oil companies have begun a process, with the acquiescence of ONHAE, that is causing irreparable harm to the forests and watersheds of Huaorani territory. Nevertheless, the leaders of ONHAE have achieved a victory of sorts in that they have at all times maintained an independent organization working (for the most part) for what they see as the immediate good of the Huaorani people. In a sense this can be compared to what Lenin (1978: 350-55) has described as a "reactionary trade union consciousness." Over time the experiences of the Huaorani leadership have given them an ever greater understanding of what can be accomplished, and how they can wield power. As stated by Christian Gros (1991: 167):

> For those who participate in the struggle, it is not enough, in the manner of other social groups, to reclaim the land, gain access to education, etc., rather, it is about affirming their capacity to guide social

change and to define their cultural system. In this case, more important than land, health or education, is the definition of an alternate
project and the possibility of controlling it. "Real" democracy and
"formal" democracy (in the manner of the indigenous people) coincide in a demand for self-determination.

But the Huaorani strategy has also served to undermine the
positions of its supposed allies in the indigenous movement. Solidarity across ethnic lines is also an important component of the
strategic planning of these indigenous groups, one that the Huaorani have at times undermined through their agreements with the
oil companies. The leadership of OPIP has been very frustrated by
these separate Huaorani agreements, which it sees as weakening its
own position in dealing with not only Maxus, but with all of the oil
companies in the region. OPIP's leadership places a very high
value on the united front of indigenous groups. Leonardo Viteri of
OPIP and the Instituto Amazanga made this clear when he stated:

> OPIP was created in 1978 under an urgent necessity for the indige-
> nous peoples of Pastaza to have an organization to count on as a valid
> switch [*interruptor*] between the indigenous peoples and the organism
> of the state. In this way to make heard our voice, our thoughts, our
> proposals and our aspirations for the future. ... In the same way, we
> can add, to establish also an international relation between our peo-
> ples . ... [T]o establish the system of cooperation, technical, economic,
> and solidarity, to support each others' proposals and give moral sup-
> port when there are problems.

An important step in moving ONHAE toward a position of
greater solidarity and consistency may have come as a result of the
1996 national elections. In these elections the national indigenous
federations chose, for the first time, to field candidates of their own
choosing in a national election (under the party name Pachakutik)
in conjunction with one of the bourgeois socialist parties (Nuevo
Pais). The Huaorani were courted by the local Pachakutik activists
and worked very closely with them, Huaorani leaders spending
many hours in the local headquarters of the party. The results of the
election were encouraging–Pachakutik became overnight the single leading opposition party in both houses of the national legis-
lature and captured numerous local posts, and the Pachakutik/
Nuevo Pais presidential candidate, Freddy Ehlers, finished third,

narrowly missing a place in the subsequent runoff voting. This political activity had a salubrious effect on the Huaorani leadership's sense of connection with the broader indigenous movement and led to many hours of discussions between Pachakutik militants and ONHAE leaders. Perhaps more importantly, the officers of ONHAE now have, in effect, direct representation in the legislative and administrative processes of the state, a connection that has brought them into closer cooperation with the other elements of the indigenous movement in the country. A reflection of this is the appointment of Armando Boya, a little more than a year after the end of my fieldwork ended, as the first Huaorani vice president of CONFENIAE, the regional federation of indigenous organizations of the *oriente*.

Another success of ONHAE, one critical to its institutional survival, has been its establishment as the undisputed legal, social, and political representative of the Huaorani people. Before peaceful contact was established there was, naturally, no one who could speak for the Huaorani. Following contact, the missionaries became the self-appointed representatives of the Huaorani, taking advantage of the ignorance and fear surrounding the Huaorani in the view of the national government. The missionaries were granted full administrative control over the Huaorani reservation, and military and other state agencies relocated hundreds of Huaorani families to the missionary-controlled lands of the "Protectorate." After the expulsion of the SIL the missionaries were stripped of the kind of juridico-political administrative control they had enjoyed previously but continued to act as representatives and spokespersons of the Huaorani for years afterward. This missionary control of the "voice" of the Huaorani became a contested terrain in the 1980s as other indigenous organizations representing Amazonian indigenous populations in Ecuador began to organize themselves effectively and attempted to speak on behalf of all of the indigenous groups in the *oriente*. Thus two ideologically opposed non-Huaorani groups claimed, for a time, to be the spokepersons of the Huaorani. Throughout this period, there was no recognized party with the legal authority to negotiate or sign agreements on behalf of the Huaorani people.[2]

Today, ONHAE has established itself as the undisputed legal representative of the Huaorani. It is constituted and registered under Ecuadorian law as the official Huaorani representative, and the organization's charter identifies it as a legal entity "with the legal capacity to sign *convenios*, contracts, and other legal instruments at the national and international level as approved by the people and organization in the realization of its objectives." In practice, anyone wishing to reach some agreement with the Huaorani always comes to ONHAE for negotiations, with the exception of Stephen Saint, who has established himself in the community of Nemonpade without the express consent of ONHAE, relying instead on his personal contacts and family connections (he is the son of Nate Saint and the nephew of Rachel Saint). The military generally defer to the wishes of the organization regarding the granting of entry permits for non-Huaorani who wish to enter the territory.[3] Newspaper reporters (Ecuadorian and international), officials of international agencies, and the Ecuadorian state (ministries of education, health, etc.) all work through ONHAE on any issue involving Huaorani territory.

ONHAE has made the maintenance of Huaorani cultural traditions one of the cornerstones of institutional policy and rhetoric. Article Two of the organization's 1992 by-laws states that "ONHAE is the struggle of the Huaorani people to maintain their culture, their rights to their lives and to their ancestral and traditional lands." Enquere, one of the founders and a former president has said that his greatest fear is that "the culture of the Huaorani people will be destroyed."

Part of the process of protecting the culture of the Huaorani has been the related process of defining the culture in its increasingly complex relationships with other groups. As we saw in the discussion of Huaorani participation in the annual 12 May parade in Puyo (Chapter 3), the Huaorani are very much aware of their image within the national/mestizo society of Ecuador, and they are not averse to using or promoting it themselves. A good example of this was the 1992 Huaorani protests in Quito, the highland capital of Ecuador, in front of the offices of Petroecuador and Maxus.[4] The Huaorani carried spears, waving them in a threatening way, painted their faces, and dressed in minimal clothing. In front of the television cameras they enhanced the "exotic" character of their presence by singing traditional Huaorani war chants and threatening to use their spears to block further entry of oil company personnel to their territory. A comparison can be made to the now famous Kayapo demonstrations at Altamira and during the Rio conference on the environment.

Gender

The very fact of organizing has encouraged or reinforced certain ongoing changes in the nature of Huaorani society particularly in the areas of gender and internal politics and decision making. In the area of gender, the organization has served to validate an already ongoing process of more rigid distinctions in the sexual division of labor. In terms of decision making processes and the structure of power in Huaorani society, ONHAE has tended to foster a greater concentration of power in the hands of a few leaders, thus weakening the traditionally diffuse and acephalous nature of Huaorani internal politics.

Traditionally, the Huaorani have had a division of labor notable among lowland peoples for its flexibility. Tasks that are predominately carried out by one or another gender are in practice frequently done by the other. Men sometimes work in the gardens or reheat food, while I have seen women hunt and help in the construction of houses and pilot canoes. Fishing, gathering firewood, and child care are very much shared duties.

But in more recent times several factors have combined that, taken together, have had the effect of making Huaorani gender roles more rigid. First, by concentrating Huaorani populations in larger and larger communities, and then making those communities permanent settlements (as a result of the need for schools, airstrips, etc.), the game in the surrounding forest areas has been quickly depleted. Consequently, when men go out to hunt it is no longer for a few hours in the morning, or even for the whole day, returning every evening to take part in the family routine; today it is normal for men to be gone for three to seven days on a hunting trip to the hinterlands of Huaorani territory. This leaves the women with the sole responsibility for the care of the household and garden. Additionally, the jobs that are intermittently available for Huaorani, providing them with the opportunity to earn wages with which to purchase food and other goods (in many ways this is just a way to make up for the scarcity of wild game) are almost exclusively for men, having the same effect as the extended hunting trips. ONHAE's leadership reflects this more rigid sexual/gender division, and this is then reinforced by the immersion of the leadership in the machismo of Ecuadorian mestizo and Quichua society, a machismo that is at its zenith in the frontier towns of the *oriente* like Puyo.

It is thus not surprising to find that up until the time of my fieldwork, through three administrations of leaders, only one woman, Nancy Guiquita had been elected to an officership in the organization, and she represents a very "special case." At the time of my fieldwork Nancy was the vice president for health of ONHAE and was replaced at the 1996 *Biye* described in Chapter 3. Nancy is the daughter of Dayuma, Rachel Saint's first "convert" to Christianity, who was set up by Rachel Saint as the dominant leader of the missionary-run communities. Nancy is married to a Quichua schoolteacher, Delfin Andy, a relatively high-status marriage, and they continue to live in the compound of buildings in Toñampade (which corresponds to a traditional *nanicabo*) belonging to Dayuma. During her tenure in office Nancy played only a marginal and marginalized role in the activities and decision making processes of the leaders of ONHAE.

No other woman has served as an officer of the organization, although Manuela Ima's position of *conserje* is an elected, though very subservient, position. At the *Biye* of 1996 women did participate actively in the discussions and in voting, and were frequently very strident in their criticisms of the current leadership, particularly in the area of education. When I attended a monthly parent teacher-meeting in Quehueire Ono mothers and grandmothers made up the bulk of those participating; only a few fathers were present.

In all, gender relations within ONHAE are a reflection of those existing in Huaorani society as it is constituted today. This represents a somewhat more androcentric structure of gender and power than that found in traditional Huaorani society, but cannot be said to be a result of the organizing process or the actions of the organization or its leadership.

Centralized Authority

One of the central theses of this work, as stated before, is that for a traditionally acephalous, egalitarian society like the Huaorani the formation of an organization with a formally established hierarchy and leaders with clearly delineated authority and responsibilities creates a nexus of power that then becomes the focus of efforts by other interested parties to influence, persuade, or co-opt the organization. The oil companies, and particularly Maxus, have focused tremendous pressure on the leaders of the organization, providing gifts, material support, and even an office staff. Some of these gifts may have taken the form of bribes to individual leaders. The environmental groups, both national and international, have devoted time and attention to the leaders of ONHAE, providing training and paying for ONHAE-sponsored events. The missionaries have offered or withheld flights, medical care, and educational grants, partly in efforts to influence the policies of the organization. The traditionally diffuse decision making practices of Huaorani society would not have been as vulnerable, I believe, to such blandishments as the ONHAE leaders have been. At a minimum, efforts to persuade the Huaorani to accept oil development would have had to have taken place at the level of individual communities, and would probably have been accompanied by some form of violent resistance and shifting demands.

The ultimate evaluation of ONHAE's early years will not be made by social scientists, but by the Huaorani people. ONHAE has effectively established itself as the representative of the Huaorani people in the eyes of the state, the press, and, I believe, the Huaorani themselves. It has executed agreements (ostensibly) on behalf of the Huaorani people and has come to be seen as a partner in the provincial, regional, and national federations of indigenous people of which it is a member. On the other hand, it has failed to maintain its stated opposition to oil development, and the agreements it has made with oil companies may in the end represent the opening wedge of a constellation of related forces that will ultimately doom the Huaorani culture and indeed the very survival of the Huaorani as a distinct ethnicity and society.

Notes

1. *Mestizaje*, the ideological construct that denies the presence of distinct ethnicities in Ecuadorian national society, claiming instead a blended *mestizo* identity, is an important part of the curriculum even in the bilingual schools of indigenous communities. For a good discussion of this question with examples see Rival 1992: 212-55, 413-18 and 420-33.
2. It should be noted that Ecuador does not possess any sort of effective "Indian protection service" comparable to the Brazilian FUNAI.
3. Officially, any foreigner or non-indigenous person entering the forests of the *oriente* is required to have a permit issued by the Ecuadorian army. In practice it is easy to enter without the permit unless one desires to fly, in which case the commercial air services all check for the permit.
4. For accounts of these events see Siracusa 1996: 192-95; Kane 1995: 226-37; and film footage in *Trinkets and Beads* 1998.

Chapter 5

CONCLUSION

A nthropology has a historic relationship with indigenous peoples. It remains the preeminent discipline in which the problems, cultures, and achievements of the "small peoples" (Lee 2000)
are studied, compared, and theorized. Despite the general shift
from the study of the peoples of the periphery to those of the met-
ropolitan nations, many anthropologists continue their work with
indigenous peoples. But there has been an important change in
these projects, as Lee (2000: 3-4) has stated:

> While many if not most Anthros [sic] have moved into the cities and
> settled there, others continue to work in the jungles of Central Amer-
> ica, the highlands of Peru, and plains of East Africa. But here the
> ground has shifted as well. It was one thing to work in these places
> when the subjects were non-literate and politically disenfranchised.
> But how do we approach peoples in the year 2000 who are politically
> articulate and who in pressing their claims hold press-conferences,
> hire lawyers, and operate web sites?

As discussed also by Nugent (1993: 230-37), the study of
indigenous peoples can no longer take the form of the study of an
individual "tribal" group. Such studies are misleading and essen-
tializing, and ignore the articulation of cultures, economies, and
systems of production. The present work represents an effort to replace indigenous peoples as an important subject for anthropological inquiry. In critically examining the struggles of indigenous

peoples, and placing the inquiry at the points of contact between two cultures, there is much to be learned about both the peripheral societies of the indigenous and the engines of historical development of the capitalist core.

The principal actors in this work include the North American evangelical missionaries, the oil companies (particularly Maxus Energy), the environmental groups (both national and international), the national and regional indigenous organizations with whom ONHAE is articulated, and the state, as well, of course, as the Huaorani themselves. ONHAE was formed in the midst of this milieu, and its trajectory of development has been shaped by the dialectical relationships between it and each of the other principal actors.

The Huaorani themselves have been portrayed as exotic savages by a variety of different actors, in many cases in order to provide a suitably exotic backdrop for the adventurous activities of different "outsiders" (cf. Broennimann 1981; Wallis 1960; Kane 1993, 1995). They inhabit the fragile tropical rainforest regions of the Ecuadorian *oriente*, where they live in extended family groups (*nanicabos*) that engage in hunting, gathering, limited slash-and-burn horticulture, and some fishing. They dwell in highland areas away from the rivers, where contacts with non-Huaorani are minimized, a settlement pattern that may indicate the adoption of some sort of refugee strategy in the distant past (this speculation is bolstered by the fact that Huao Terero is a linguistic isolate). Certainly before the 1960s, the Huaorani people were fearful of and hostile to any outsider entering their territory. Huaorani culture is notable for its fluidity and pliability–gender roles, foods, and codes of behavior are shifting and flexible and internal social relations are generally harmonious. Prior to contact with western missionaries, the Huaorani were known (and feared) primarily for the notorious violence that characterized relations between themselves and any *cowode* who entered their territory.

The history of the Huaorani people in the twentieth century is a catalogue of destructive contacts with non-Huaorani. The rubber boom of the turn of the century was succeeded by the penetration of the first oil exploration teams, which in turn were followed by the evangelical missionaries of the Summer Institute of Linguistics and other groups. The missionaries of the SIL were right-wing ethnocidal agents of American hegemony. Preaching an anti-Semitic, antipluralist, and intolerant version of Christianity, they were nevertheless granted complete control over a reservation for the Huaorani by the Ecuadorian government. This they achieved by falsely claiming to be a scientific organization devoted to the study of linguistics (the cornerstone of SIL strategy). Allying themselves with the oil interests, the missionaries have facilitated the entry of the oil companies into the region and have actively discouraged the Huaorani from effectively organizing.

After the missionaries–and allied with them–came the oil companies. Initially in territories to the north of the Huaorani, then moving inside Huaorani territory itself in the 1980s, the oil companies began the processes of exploration, seismic tests, and finally well drilling. The lands of the Huaorani were divided into exploration blocks by the Ecuadorian government and auctioned off. First Conoco, then Maxus, and today Oryx, YPF, and Petrobras purchased rights to some part of Huaorani territory. The process of oil exploration and extraction, as well as its accompanying road and pipeline building, is inherently destructive of natural environments under the best of circumstances in the developed world. In Ecuador and throughout the less developed world the process has been one of terrible and unrelieved devastation.

The Huaorani have always been an isolated group. Their language is unrelated to other known indigenous languages in the region. They have not engaged in significant trade or intermarried with neighboring indigenous populations, and they have traditionally responded with violence to any non-Huaorani attempting to enter their territory. Yet today the Huaorani have adopted the strident rhetoric of solidarity and struggle of the national indigenous movement, depicting all indigenous peoples of Ecuador as "brothers." ONHAE has emulated organizational forms, rhetoric, and strategies developed by the organizations representing other indigenous groups. Nevertheless, tensions and jealousies remain, and impede the full articulation of ONHAE with the broader indigenous movement in Ecuador.

ONHAE is a particularly interesting case for anthropology to examine. The Huaorani have experienced only limited contact with non-Huaorani, and only over a little more than one generation. The mode of production still existing among the Huaorani people is an egalitarian primitive communism. Yet this acephalous, scattered, and isolated group has chosen the most formal of possible responses to the encroachment of capitalism and the concomitant threats to their society. By choosing a formal organization, and articulating themselves with the broadest and strongest national indigenous movement in all of Latin America, the Huaorani have attempted to secure their rights and a space for (at least partly) self-determined cultural change through an organizational structure modeled after those of other indigenous activist groups. As this process has unfolded the Huaorani have found themselves involved in a plethora of unanticipated conflicts, issues, and arenas of struggle, while simultaneously making what their leaders see as pragmatic retreats from the most fundamental positions taken at the time of the group's founding.

The relationships between the Huaorani organization and other parties is not one of simple oppositions and alliances. It is too easy to view ONHAE as the opponent of the oil companies, or the ally (however flawed) of the environmental or indigenous-rights movements. ONHAE is positioned in the midst of a number of interests, each pursuing a different agenda. ONHAE's positions and policies with respect to each of these groups are contingent, shifting, and flexible, in a manner analogous to the flexibility and pliancy of roles and positions within Huaorani society. Strategic alliances are continually formed and broken as the leadership of ONHAE attempts to balance these competing claims to their loyalties and policy goals.

ONHAE's record, discussed in the previous chapter, is one that has left many observers and potential allies dissatisfied. ONHAE has gained the support of a variety of different activist groups, each with somewhat different motivations. Each of the principal allies involved in the creation of ONHAE–the environmental movement, the indigenous rights organizations, and others, all saw ONHAE primarily as a weapon in the struggle against the oil companies penetration of the *oriente*. The strong position against oil development taken by the organization at the beginning has been eroded as the group's leaders have continued to permit the oil exploitation of Huaorani territory to proceed. This, in turn, has impacted every other activity undertaken by the organization.

Money from the oil company makes possible the ONHAE office and staff, the *linderación* (border marking project), and the health and education initiatives. ONHAE's agreements with the oil companies have strained relations between the organization and the indigenous and environmental movements. Simultaneously, the Huaorani leadership have learned to use their public alliances with the environmental and indigenous movements as a source of leverage to extract greater concessions from the oil companies. They have also learned to successfully extract cash and services from some of the groups opposed to oil development, as seen when the Rainforest Action Network helped to pay for the 1996 *Biye* in Toñampade.

By forming a legally responsible, hierarchical, and all-encompassing (i.e., pan-Huaorani) organization, the founders of ONHAE unwittingly created a concentration of power over the administration of Huaorani lands such as the Huaorani had never before possessed. This power was concentrated, in emulation of the rules for the governing bodies of other Ecuadorian indigenous groups, in the hands of a discrete cadre of officers who, though popularly elected, exercised a great amount of individual discretion in decisionmaking and policy implementation and who, during their term of office, work in an environment far removed, both physically and spiritually, from the forest home of the Huaorani. The result of this concentration of authority was that the oil companies and other interested parties were able to focus all of their efforts to persuade, suborn, or entice the Huaorani on a small group of no more than ten individuals whose decision would be dispositive of the fate of the forest.

Huaorani relations with the state were problematic. It is the policy of the Ecuadorian government to encourage oil development and to facilitate the process of oil company penetration of the region. At the same time, the state is sensitive to criticism (particularly from international sources) of its environmental and human rights records, and the Huaorani are able to draw attention to themselves because of their "fame" as a "stone age tribe." In the past the state had chosen to withdraw from the area, handing control over to the missionaries of the SIL, but with the growth in oil exploration's importance in the Ecuadorian economy the state began to take on a much greater role in the territory. An arena for new investigation is the possible change in relations with the state now that the party formed by the indigenous movement has come to play such a significant role in national politics.

Most importantly, the opposition faced by ONHAE in its efforts to secure the future of the Huaorani people has shaped the structure and behavior of the organization and its leadership. Unlike the Kayapo, who confront a variety of petty capitalist loggers and gold miners, each mounting an individual effort to co-opt the Kayapo leaders, the Huaorani must confront a nearly monolithic oil enterprise—one with unlimited resources (at least when seen in the regional context of the Ecuadorian *oriente*), coordinated activities, and the ability to assign professionals whose only job is the persuasion or co-optation of the indigenous leadership; an industry with the clear support of the government of Ecuador and the court system. In part, this reflects the organic composition of capital of the different capitalist enterprises. Oil development requires a vast outlay of capital in the form of machinery and technology, with relatively little labor being necessary in the immediate processes of production in the forest (capital machinery may represent stored labor power); this necessitates economies of scale and large enterprises engaging in large-scale production.

ONHAE has given the Huaorani people a voice in conflicts with the state. This voice is, for the first time in Huaorani post-contact history, not one that is filtered through the pro-capitalist, pro-development, foreign evangelical missionaries. The organization actively represents Huaorani interests in conflicts with the state, the other indigenous federations, and the missionaries. The leadership has made compromises, under tremendous pressure, with the oil interests, thus permitting the penetration of extractive capitalism in Huaorani territory. In permitting the oil companies to enter their territory ONHAE has wrung concessions from the oil companies, but these have been (from the standpoint of the oil industry) insignificant gifts rather than substantial royalties or long-term aid.

The practice of ONHAE is still evolving. Leaders rely heavily on the advice and guidance of non-Huaorani, including the organization's own staff, in the implementation of policy. This reliance on input from outsiders may contribute to the leadership's vulnerability to the oil interests' efforts to influence and co-opt them. The leadership lives and works away from Huaorani territory, and remains distanced and remote from the rank-and-file of Huaorani communities–a source of frequent discussion and complaint during the *Biye*. The organization has played an important role in the nascent development of a pan-Huaorani consciousness–the process that has been described as a key component of ethnogenesis.

ONHAE's internal decisionmaking processes are dominated by the *Biye*, the paramount authority of the organization. This institution, deliberately linked to a reimagined past, is an extraordinarily democratic reflection of traditional Huaorani group process, overlain with borrowed practices and formalities. The leaders are loath to challenge the authority of the *Biye*, or to deny its legitimacy or its right to meet, but in practice the members of the leadership often reinterpret the resolutions and policies of the *Biye* to give themselves greater flexibility in negotiations and to avoid alienating any of the group's potential backers. The institutionalized positions of the leaders of the organization represent something new in the Huaorani context. The concentration of authority in the hands of a small group such as these officers is antithetical to Huaorani traditions and, particularly when juxtaposed with the deeply rooted desire of the leadership to contribute to or share with the broader community, makes the leaders easy prey to offers of gifts or assistance to the outlying communities for which they can take credit.

ONHAE has succeeded in establishing itself as the recognized voice of the Huaorani people. It has achieved official recognition as the legal representative of the Huaorani, with the recognized right to negotiate and sign contracts on behalf of the Huaorani people. It has succeeded as well in guaranteeing a form of territorial integrity, albeit with some large loopholes. It has also succeeded in extracting (or gathering?) significant assistance for Huaorani education, health, and border marking projects, and for the maintenance and reproduction of the organization itself. It has successfully retained its own institutional independence, even while articulating with the regional and national indigenous movements and, now, a political party of the left opposition. However, ONHAE has made a series of agreements with the international oil companies operating in and around Huaorani territory. These agreements, apart from the environmental and social damage that will be caused by oil development, have placed a great strain on the natural allies of the Huaorani: the indigenous organizations, the environmental movement, and the anti-imperialist left.

The unanswered question implicit in this work remains. What is the most effective way for indigenous peoples to organize in the face of capitalist penetration? More broadly, how is it most possible for the dispossessed of the periphery (indigenous or non) to claim rights and develop a voice against oppression? In the 1960s much of the Latin American left took a "vanguardist" approach, attempting to build left parties and guerrilla movements that transcended, and in practice denied, the differing interests of competing sectors of society, including feminism, *indigenismo*, and others (cf. Huberman and Sweezy 1968; Hawley 1997). Today a new strategic agreement is emerging within the Latin American left. As stated by Chinchilla (1992: 49): "For Latin American Marxists, for example, the hope of overthrowing corrupt, unpopular, and elite-based authoritarian regimes as a result of the efforts of a small but dedicated clandestine guerrilla band has been exchanged for the growing consensus that the power of entrenched privileged elites and their external allies can only be overcome by the broadest, most democratic grass-roots movement possible."

The new strategic consensus finds expression in the development and articulation of groups with differing political analyses and outlooks, different strategies, and different racial, class, or gender identifications (for discussion see Gros 1991: 158-67; Chinchilla 1992: 37-51). In Ecuador this new-style movement has found expression in a number of struggles ranging from the establishment of Pachakutik, a political party that has linked the white and mestizo intellectuals of the democratic left with the long-established Ecuadorian indigenous rights movements, to the popular uprisings that overthrew the appallingly corrupt Ecuadorian President Abdala Bucaram in 1997-98—a movement in which women's groups, indigenous organizations, and trade unions joined with the traditional left parties and student groups in a general strike and street mobilizations that toppled the government and led to a new constitution.

Mobilizations against entrenched power are being mounted increasingly by activists and groups representing relatively narrowly defined interests or constituencies. This has meant that peoples' movements are built on diffuse, contingent, shifting, and sometimes contradictory coalitions. The independent participation of ONHAE in these national and transnational arenas represents a real and progressive step toward a sort of self-determination. But the concentration of power in the hands of a small cadre of leaders has proven to be a less than ideal way of providing the sort of internal governance needed by the organization.

WORKS CITED

Acción Ecologica. 1994. *Amazonia por la Vida: Guia Ambiental para la Defensa del Territorio Amazonico Amenazado por las Petroleras.* Quito: Acción Ecologica.

Acción Ecologica. 1995. *Amazonia por la Vida: Derechos de las Poblaciones Amazónicas Frente a la Actividad Petrolera (Leyes y Procidimientos Juridicos).* Quito: Acción Ecologica.

Bamat, Tomás. 1986. *¿Salvación ó Dominación?: Las Sectas Religiosas en el Ecuador.* Quito: Editorial El Conejo.

Bartolomé, Miguel A. 1995. *Ya No Hay Lugar Para Cazadores: Procesos de extinción y Transfiguración Etnica en América Latina.* Quito: Abya-Yala.

Bocco, Arnaldo. 1987. *Auge Petrolero, Modernización Y Subdesarollo.* Quito: Corporación Editora Nacional.

Bradby, Barbara. 1980. "The Destruction of the Natural Economy." In *The Articulation of the Modes of Production,* edited by Harold Wolpe, pp. 93-127. London: Routledge and Kegan Paul.

Broennimann, Peter. 1981. *Auca on the Cononaco.* Boston: Birkhauser Publishers.

Brown, Michael F., and Margaret L. Van Bolt. 1980. "Aguaruna Jivaro Gardening Magic in the Alto Rio Mayo, Peru." *Ethnology* 19, 2: 169-90.

Cabodevilla, Miguel Angel. 1994. *Los Huaorani en la Historia de los Pueblos del Oriente.* Coca, Ecuador: CICAME.

Cano, Ginette, Karl Neufeldt, Heinz Schulze, Waltraud Schulze-Vogel, Norbert Georg, M. José Van de Loo, Kaethe Meentzen. 1981. *Los Nuevos Conquistadores: El Instituto Lingüístico de Verano en America Latina.* Quito: CEDIS/FENOC.

Centro para Derechos Economicos y Sociales. 1994. *Violaciones de Derechos en la Amazonia Ecuatoriana: Las consecuencias Humanas del Desarollo Petrolero.* Quito: Abya-Yala.

Chagnon, Napoleon A. 1992. *Yanomamö*. New York: Harcourt Brace Jovanovich.

Chinchilla, Norma Stoltz. 1992. "Marxism, Feminism, and the Struggle for Democracy In Latin America." In *The Making of Social Movements in Latin America,* Edited by Arturo Escobar and Sonia Alvarez, pp. 37-51. Boulder, CO: Westview Press.

Colby, Gerard, and Charlotte Dennett. 1995. *Thy Will Be Done: The Conquest of the Amazon, Nelson Rockefeller and Evangelism in the Age of Oil.* New York: HarperCollins.

Compte, Francisco Maria. 1885. *Varones Ilustres de la Orden Serafica en el Ecuador Desde la Fundación de Quito Hasta Nuestros Días*. Vol. 1, Quito: Imprenta del Clero.

CONAIE. 1989. *Las Nacionalidades Indigenas en el Ecuador: Nuestro Proceso Organativo*. Quito: Abya-Yala.

CONFENIAE. 1995. *Voz de la CONFENIAE,* no. 16.

Conklin, Elizabeth A. 1994. "War Clubs, Feathers and VCR's: Technology and Rainforest Politics in Brazil." Paper presented at the annual meeting of the American Anthropological Association, Washington, D.C.

_____. 1999. "Absent Presences: The Problem of Mourning in Amazonian Mourning." Paper presented at the annual meeting of the American Anthropoogical Association, Chicago, Illinois.

Cornejo Menacho, Diego, ed. 1993. *Los Indios y el Estado Pais: Pluriculturidad y Multietnicidad en el Ecuador*. Quito: Abya-Yala.

Cueva, Augustín. 1982. *The Process of Political Domination in Ecuador*. New Brunswick, N.J: Transaction Press.

Dall'Alba B., Leonir. 1992. *Pioneros, Nativos y Colonos: El Dorado en el Siglo XX*. Quito: Abya-Yala.

Delgado, Guillermo P. 1996. " Entre lo Popular y lo Etnico: Notas de un Debate Para un Debate." In *Pueblos Indios, Soberanía y Globalismo,* edited by Stefano Varese, pp. 31-80. Quito: Abya-Yala.

Eckstein, Susan, ed. 1989. *Power and Popular Protest: Latin American Social Movements*. Berkeley: University of California.

Elliot, Elisabeth. 1966. *No Graven Image*. London: Hodder and Stoughton Ltd..

_____. 1970 [1958]. *Shadow of the Almighty: The Life and Testament of Jim Elliot*. Grand Rapids: Zondervan Publishing.

_____. 1981 [1956]. *Through Gates of Splendor*. Wheaton, Ill.: Living Books.

Escobar, Arturo, and Sonia Alvarez. 1992. *The Making of Social Movements in Latin America*. Boulder: Westview Press.

Fuentes, Bertha. 1997. *Huaomoni, Huarani, Cowudi: Una Aproximación a los Huaorani en la Practica Politica Multi-étnica Ecuatoriana*. Quito: Abya Yala.

Galeano, Eduardo. 1997. *Las Venas Abiertas de América Latina*. Mexico, D.F.: Siglo Veintiuno.

Gledhill, John. 1994. *Power and its Disguises: Anthropological Perspectives on Politics*. Boulder: Pluto Press.

Goffin, Alvin M. 1994. *The Rise of Protestant Evangelism in Ecuador, 1895-1990*. Gainesville: Fla.: University Press of Florida.

Gomez, Nelson, coordinator. 1992. *Tempestad en la Amazonia Ecuatoriana*. Quito: Editorial Ediguias.

Gray, Andrew. 1997. *Indigenous Rights and Development: Self-Determination in an Amazonian Community*. Providence: Berghahn Books.

Gros, Christian. 1991. *Colombia Indígena*. Bogotá: Fondo Editorial CEREC.

Hallum, Anne Motley. 1996. *Beyond Missionaries: Toward an Understanding of the Protestant Movement in Central America*. New York: Rowman and Littlefield.

Hanratty, Dennis M., et al. 1991. *Ecuador: A Country Study*. Washington, D.C.: Library of Congress.

Hawley, Susan. 1997. "Protestantism and Indigenous Mobilization: The Moravian Church Among the Miskito Indians of Nicaragua." *Journal of Latin American Studies*. 29,1; (February).

Hecht, Susanna, and Alexander Cockburn. 1989. *The Fate of the Forest: Developers, Destoyers and Defenders of the Amazon*. New York: Verso.

Hefner, Robert W., ed. 1993. *Conversion to Christianity: Historical and Anthropological Perspectives on a Great Transformation*. Berkeley: University of California.

Hill, Jonathan D. 1999. "The Mythic Primordium Enters Pentium Space-Time." Paper presented at the annual meeting of the American Anthropological Association, Chicago, Illinois.

Hitt, Russell T. 1975 [1959]. *Jungle Pilot: The Life and Witness of Nate Saint*. Grand Rapids: Zondervan.

Hoy. 1995. "Indígenas Piden Mayor Participacion." 21 April, p. 5-A.

Hurtado, Osvaldo. 1985. *Political Power in Ecuador*. Boulder: Westview Press.

Huberman, Leo, and Paul M. Sweezy, eds. 1968. *Regis Debray and the Latin American Revolution*. New York: Monthly Review.

Hvalkof, Søren, and Peter Aaby, eds. 1981. *Is God an American?* Copenhagen: International Work Group for Indigenous Affairs.

Jackson, Dave, and Neta Jackson. 1997. *The Fate of the Yellow Woodbee.* Minneapolis: Bethany House Publishers.

Kane, Joe. 1993. "With Spears From All Sides." *The New Yorker* (27 September): 54-79.

_____. 1994. "Moi Goes to Washington". *The New Yorker* (2 May): 74-81.

_____. 1995. *Savages.* New York: Alfred A. Knopf.

Kaplan, Jonathan E., et al. 1984. "Workup on the Waorani." *Natural History* 9,84:69-74.

Kensinger, Kenneth M. 1995. *How Real People Ought to Live: The Cashinahua of Eastern Peru.* Prospect Heights, Ill.: Waveland Press.

Kimmerling, Judith. 1991. *Amazon Crude.* New York: National Resources Defense Council.

Labaca, Alejandro. 1993. *Cronica Huaorani.* Pompeya, Napo, Ecuador: Ediciones CICAME.

Lee, Richard B. 2000. "Indigenism and Its Discontents: Anthropology and the Small Peoples at the Millenium." Keynote address presented to the 2000 meetings of the American Ethnological Society.

Lenin, V. I. 1978. *On Trade Unions.* Moscow: Progress Publishers.

Lewis, Norman. 1988. *The Missionaries: God Against the Indians.* New York: Penguin Books.

Lowie, Robert. 1961 [1920]. *Primitive Society.* New York: Harper Torchbooks.

Lyon, Patricia J. 1985. *Native South Americans: Ethnology of the Least Known Continent.* Prospect Heights, Ill.: Waveland Press.

MacDonald, Theodore. 1995a. "Ecuadorian Amazonian Indigenous Organizations: Ethnic-Based Social Movements as Responses to Domination." Proposal submitted to the Harry Frank Guggenheim Foundation.

_____. 1995b. "Changing Views of Land, Resources, and Self: Indigenous Latin American Social Movements in the 1990s." Program on Nonviolent Sanctions and Cultural Survival Seminar Synopses: http://data.fas.harvard.edu/cfia/pnscs/ DOCS/s95macdo.htm.

Man, John. 1982. *Jungle Nomads of Ecuador: The Waorani.* Amsterdam: Time-Life Books.

Martz, John D. 1987. *Politics and Petroleum in Ecuador.* New Brunswick, N.J: Transaction Books.

Marx, Karl, and Friedrich Engels. 1967 [1848]. *The Communist Manifesto.* New York: Seabury Press.

Maybury-Lewis, David. 1997. *Indigenous Peoples, Ethnic Groups, and the State.* Boston: Allyn and Bacon.

Meggers, Betty J. 1996. *Amazonia: Man and Culture in a Counterfeit Paradise.* Washington, D.C.: Smithsonian Institution Press.

Mera, J., Wilson Humberto, and Valther Ernesto Montaño T. 1984. *Colonización de la Región Amazónica en el Desarrollo Capitalista.* Quito: Editorial Universitario.

Miller, Elmer. 1970. "The Christian Missionary, Agent of Secularization." *Anthropological Quarterly* 43,1: 14-22.

Moore, Thomas R. 1981. "SIL and a 'New-found Tribe': The Amarakaeri Experience." In *Is God an American?* edited by Søren Hvalkof and Peter Aaby, pp. 133-44. Copenhagen: International Work Group for Indigenous Affairs.

Moran, Emilio F. 1993. *Through Amazonian Eyes: The Human Ecology of Amazonian Populations.* Iowa City: University of Iowa Press.

Muratorio, Blanca. 1981. "Protestantism and Capitalism Revisited in the Rural Highlands of Ecuador." *Journal of Peasant Studies* 8,1: 37-60.

_____. 1982. *Etnicidad. Evangelización y Protesta en el Ecuador.* Quito: Centro de Investigaciones y Estudios Socio-Económicos.

_____. 1991. *The Life and Times of Grandfather Alonso.* New Brunswick, N.J.: Rutgers.

_____, ed. 1994. *Imágenes e Imagineros.* Quito: FLACSO.

Murdock, George Peter. 1974. "South American Culture Areas." In *Native South Americans: Ethnology of the Least Known Continent,* edited by Patricia Lyon. Prospect Heights, Ill.: Waveland Press.

Newson, Linda A. 1995. *Life and Death in Early Colonial Ecuador.* Norman, Okla.: University of Oklahoma Press.

Nugent, Stephen. 1993. *Amazonian Caboclo Society: An Essay on Invisibility and Peasant Economy.* Providence: Berg.

Palomino, Cebero, ed. 1980. *El ILV: Un Fraude.* Lima: Ediciones Rupa Rupa.

Patterson, Thomas C. 1993. *Archaeology: The Historical Development of Civilizations.* Englewood Cliffs, N.J.: Prentice Hall.

_____. 2000. *Change and Development in the Twentieth Century.* New York: Berg.

Pérez, Gloria, and Scott Robinson. 1983. *La Misión Detrás de la Misión.* Mexico, D.F.: Claves Latinoamericanos – COPEC/CECOPE y CADAL.

Place, Susan E., ed. 1993. *Tropical Rainforests: Latin American Nature and Society in Transition.* Wilmington: Jaguar Books.

Poblacion Indigena Y Desarollo Amazonico. 1987. Quito: Abya-Yala.

Pollack, Donald K. 1993. "Conversion and 'Community' in Amazonia." In *Conversion to Christianity: Historical and Anthropological Perspectives on a Great Transformation,* edited by Robert W. Hefner, pp. 165-98. Berkeley: University of California Press.

Price, David. 1989. *Before the Bulldozer: The Nambiquara Indians and the World Bank.* Washington, D.C.: Seven Locks Press.

Rabben, Linda. 1998. *Unnatural Selection: The Yanomami, the Kayapó and the Onslaught of Civilisation.* Seattle: University of Washington Press.

Ramos, Alcida Rita. 1994. "The Hyperreal Indian." *Critique of Anthropology* 14,2: 153-172.

Reid, Daniel, ed. 1990. *Dictionary of Christianity in America.* Downers Grove, Ill.: Intervarsity Press.

Reid, Jan. 1995. "Crude Awakening." *Texas Monthly* (November): 140+.

Rival, Laura. 1992. *Social Transformations and the Impact of Formal Schooling on the Huaorani of Amazonian Ecuador.* Unpublished Ph.D. dissertation, London School of Economics.

———. 1994. "Los Indígenas Huaorani en la Conciencia Nacional: Alteridad Representada y Significada." In *Imágenes e Imageneros: Representaciones de los Indígenas Ecuatorianos, Siglos XIX y XX,* edited by Blanca Muratorio, pp. 253-92. Quito: FLACSO.

———. 1998. "The Growth of Family Trees: Understanding Huaorani Perceptions of the Forest". *Man,* 28: 635-52.

Robarchek, Clayton, and Carole Robarchek. 1998. *Waorani: The Contexts of Violence and War.* Philadelphia: Harcourt Brace.

Robinson, Scott. 1971. "Algunos Aspectos de la Colonizacion Espontanea de las Sociedades Selvaticas Ecuatorianas." In *La Situación del Indígena en America del Sur* edited by Georg Grunberg, 127-53. Montevideo: Tierra Nueva.

Saint, Steve. 1996. "Did They Have to Die?" *Christianity Today.* 40,10: 20.

Scott, James C. 1990. *Domination and the Arts of Resistance: Hidden Transcripts.* New Haven, Conn.: Yale.

Selverston, Melina H. 1995. "The Politics of Culture: Indigenous Peoples and the State in Ecuador." In *Indigenous Peoples and Democracy in Latin America,* edited by Donna Lee Van Cott, pp. 131-54. New York: St. Martin's Press.

Siracusa, Christina Angelina. 1996. *Transnational Dimensions of Ethnic Politics: A Comparative Study of the Shuar and Huaorani of the Ecuadorian Amazon.* Ph.D. dissertation, The Johns Hopkins University.

Smith, Randy. 1993. *Crisis Under the Canopy/Drama Bajo el Manto Amazonico.* Quito: Abya-Yala.

Sorensen, Arthur P. Jr. 1967. "Multilingualism in the Northwest Amazon." *American Anthropologist* 69: 670-84.

Sponsel, Leslie E., ed. 1995. *Indigenous Peoples and the Future of Amazonia: An Ecological Anthropology of an Endangered World.* Tuscon: University of Arizona Press.

———. 1995. "Relationships Among the World System, Indigenous Peoples, and Ecological Anthropology in the endangered Amazon." In *Indigenous Peoples and the Future of Amazonia: An Ecological Anthropology of an Endangered World,* edited by Leslie E. Sponsel. Tuscon: University of Arizona Press.

Steward, Julian H., and Louis C. Faron. 1959. *Native Peoples of South America.* New York: McGraw-Hill.

Stoll, David. 1982. *Fishers of Men or Founders of Empire: The Wycliffe Bible Translators in Latin America.* London: Zed Press.

Swanson, Jeffrey. 1995. *Echoes of the Call: Identity and Ideology Among American Missionaries in Ecuador.* New York: Oxford University Press.

Talbott, Hudson, and Mark Greenberg. 1996. *Amazon Diary.* New York: G. P. Putnum's Sons.

Tarrow, Sidney. 1994. *Power in Movement: Social Movements, Collective Action and Politics.* New York: Cambridge University Press.

Taylor, Anne-Christine. 1994. "Una Categoría Irreductible en el Conjunto de las Naciones Indígenas: Los Jívaro en las Representaciones Occidentales." In *Imágenes e Imagineros: Representaciones de los Indígenas Ecuatorianos, Siglos XIX y XX,* edited by Blanca Muratorio, pp. 75-108. Quito: FLACSO.

Terray, Emmanuel. 1972. *Marxism and "Primitive" Societies.* New York: Monthly Review.

Turner, Terence. 1992. "Defiant Images: The Kayapo Appropriation of Video", *Anthropology Today* 8, 6 (December).

———. 1995. "The Kayapo Revolt Against Extractivism: An Indigenous People's Struggle for Socially Eqitable and Ecologically Sustainable Production". (publication forthcoming).

Urban, Greg, and Joel Sherzer. 1988. "The linguistic Anthropology of Native South America." *Annual Review of Anthropology* 17: 283-307.

———. 1991. *Nation States and Indians in Latin America.* Austin, Tx.: University of Texas Press.

Urban, Greg. 1991. "The Semiotics of State-Indian Linguistic Relationships: Peru, Paraguay, and Brazil." In *Nation States and Indians in Latin America,* editied by Greg Urban and Joel Sherzer. Austin, Tx.: University of Texas Press.

Van Cott, Donna Lee, ed.. 1995. *Indigenous Peoples and Democracy in Latin America.* New York: St. Martin's Press.

Varea, Anamaría. 1995. *Marea Negra en la Amazonia: Conflictos Socioambientales Vinculados a la Actividad Petrolera en el Ecuador.* Quito: Abya-Yala/ILDIS.

Varese, Stefano. 1996. *Pueblos Indios, Soberanía y Globalismo.* Quito: Abya-Yala.

Villamil, Hector. 1995. "El Manejo del conflicto con las Petroleras: El caso de la ARCO-OPIP." In *Marea Negra en la Amazonia,* edited by Anamaría Varea, pp. 339-66. Quito: Abya-Yala/ILDIS.

Wallis, Ethel E. 1960. *The Dayuma Story: Life Under Auca Spears.* New York: Harper Bros.

Warren, Kay B. 1998. *Indigenous Movements and Their Critics: Pan Maya Activism in Guatemala.* Princeton N.J.: Princeton University Press.

Whitten, Norman. 1976. *Sacha Runa: Ethnicity and Adaptation of Ecuadorian Jungle Quichua.* Chicago: University of Illinois Press.

_____, ed. 1981. *Cultural Transformations and Ethnicity in Modern Ecuador.* Chicago: University of Illinois Press.

_____. 1985. *Sicuanga Runa: The Other Side Of Development in Amazonian Ecuador.* Chicago: University of Illinois Press.

Wolpe, Harold, ed. 1980. *The Articulation of Modes of Production.* London: Routledge and Kegan Paul.

Wood, Charles H. 1983. "Peasant and Capitalist Production in the Brazilian Amazon: A Conceptual Framework for the Study of Frontier Expansion." In *The Dilemma of Amazonian Development,* edited by Emilio F. Moran, pp 259-278. Boulder: Westview Press.

Worsley, Peter. 1968. *The Trumpet Shall Sound.* New York: Schocken Books.

Yost, James A. and Patricia M. Kelley. 1983. "Shotguns, Blowguns, and Spears: The Analysis of Technological Efficiency" In *Adaptive Responses of Native Amazonians,* edited by Raymond Hames and Edward Vickers, pp. 189 – 224 New York: Academic Press.

Yost, James A. 1981a. "Twenty Years of Contact: The Mechanisms of Change in Wao "Auca" Culture." In *Cultural Transformations and Ethnicity in Modern Ecuador,* edited by Norman E. Whitten, pp. 677-704. Urbana: U. of Illinois Press.

_____. 1981b. "The Waorani", IN *Ecuador: In the Shadow of the Volcanoes,* pp 97–115 Venice: Centro Studi Ricerche Ligabue.

INDEX

Printed in the United States
67158LVS00003B/1-99